# Sustainable Health Promotion Practices and the Global Economy

This book reviews the strategies for the development of sustainable health promotion practices, including the Sustainable Development Goals (SDGs), with case examples from the COVID-19 pandemic.

Beginning with a historical survey of the global agenda of health promotion over the past decades, the book analyses the evolving standards, goals and strategies of health promotion as well as the challenges encountered in implementing health promotion practices during the COVID-19 pandemic. Both social and environmental determinants of population health are examined here. Contributors have assessed socio-economic inequalities present in health promotion practices and highlighted the need for balance between economic development and financial sustainability in health services and educational programming. A framework for improved lifelong population health for all is also suggested.

This review of social, economic, environmental, and ecological contexts in health promotion will be of interest to policymakers, academics, and practitioners. In particular, scholars of health policy and health promotion, as well as public administration and development studies, will find this a useful volume.

**Ben Y. F. Fong** is Professor of Practice (Health Studies) and Director of the Centre for Ageing and Healthcare Management Research at the College of Professional and Continuing Education of The Hong Kong Polytechnic University, Hong Kong, China.

**Wang-Kin Chiu** is a senior lecturer at the College of Professional and Continuing Education of The Hong Kong Polytechnic University, Hong Kong, China.

## Routledge Studies in the Modern World Economy

**Inequality and Public Policy**
Towards Visible Equality and Equal Opportunity
*Bhanoji Rao, Suresh K.G. and Pundarik Mukhopadhaya*

**The Governance of Economic Development**
Investment, Innovation, and Competition in China
*Anson Au*

**The Economics of Russia's War in Ukraine**
Impact Analysis of Economic Policy and Finance
*Nataliya Struk, Maryana Prokop and Oleksandra Struk*

**Cybersecurity, Law and Economics**
The Case of India
*Edited by Dr. Gagandeep Kaur, Dr. Narendra N. Dalei, Dr. Sushanta Kumar Mahapatra and Dr. Vinay Kandpal*

**International Economic Policy for the Polycrisis**
*Edited by Konrad Raczkowski and Piotr Komorowski*

**Mega-Regional Trade Agreements and India**
Balancing Economic and Strategic Concerns
*Pankhuri Gaur*

**Wealth-Power Dialectic**
China's New Economic Statecraft
*Zhang Xiaotong*

**Sustainable Health Promotion Practices and the Global Economy**
*Edited by Ben Y. F. Fong and Wang-Kin Chiu*

For more information about this series, please visit: www.routledge.com/Routledge-Studies-in-the-Modern-World-Economy/book-series/SE0432

# Sustainable Health Promotion Practices and the Global Economy

Edited by Ben Y. F. Fong
and Wang-Kin Chiu

Routledge
Taylor & Francis Group
LONDON AND NEW YORK

First published 2025
by Routledge
4 Park Square, Milton Park, Abingdon, Oxon OX14 4RN

and by Routledge
605 Third Avenue, New York, NY 10158

*Routledge is an imprint of the Taylor & Francis Group, an informa business*



*British Library Cataloguing-in-Publication Data*
A catalogue record for this book is available from the British Library

ISBN: 978-1-032-70132-5 (hbk)
ISBN: 978-1-032-70133-2 (pbk)
ISBN: 978-1-032-70135-6 (ebk)

DOI: 10.4324/9781032701356

Typeset in Galliard
by Apex CoVantage, LLC

# Contents

# Biographies of Lead Authors and Contributors

**Ben Y. F. Fong** graduated in Medicine from the University of Sydney, Australia, where he also obtained his master's degree in public health. He had his clinical training at the Royal Prince Alfred Hospital in Sydney and had later held a senior management position at Prince Henry Hospital, a teaching hospital of the University of New South Wales. He is Specialist in Community Medicine, holding Honorary Clinical Associate Professorship at the two local medical schools in Hong Kong, China. He is currently Professor of Practice (Health Studies) and Associate Division Head of the Division of Science, Engineering and Health Studies, and Centre Director of the Centre for Ageing and Healthcare Management Research, of the College of Professional and Continuing Education, The Hong Kong Polytechnic University. He is also Adjunct Associate Professor of the Hong Kong Institute of Integrated Medicine at The Chinese University of Hong Kong and Adjunct Professor in Public Health & Tropical Medicine at the College of Public Health, Medical and Veterinary Sciences at James Cook University, Queensland, Australia. He has contributed to publications as lead editor of books in English, including the *Routledge Handbook of Public Health and the Community* and *Sustainable Development Goal 3 – Health and Well-being of Ageing in Hong Kong* in 2021, over 30 health books in Chinese, 40 book chapters, and 70 journal papers.

**Wang-Kin Chiu** received his Bachelor of Science (first-class honours) and a PhD in Chemistry from The Chinese University of Hong Kong, China. He is Senior Lecturer at the College of Professional and Continuing Education (CPCE) of The Hong Kong Polytechnic University (PolyU). He is currently serving as the Programme Leader of Associate in Health Studies and the Assistant Award Leader of Bachelor of Science (Honours) in Applied Sciences (Health Studies). Dr Chiu is also Management Committee Member of the Centre for Ageing and Healthcare Management Research (CAHMR) of CPCE at PolyU. He has published journal papers and book chapters related to an ageing population and sustainable environment.

## Contributors

**Nicole W. Y. Fung** is a graduate of the Bachelor of Science (Honours) in Applied Sciences (Health Studies) from the School of Professional Education and Executive Development of The Hong Kong Polytechnic University. She is Associate Fellow of the Hong Kong College of Community Health Practitioners.

**Sherry Fung** is currently Research Assistant at the Hong Kong Institute of Integrative Medicine at The Chinese University of Hong Kong, China. She is First Class Honours graduate of the Bachelor of Science (Honours) in Applied Sciences (Health Studies) from the School of Professional Education and Executive Development of The Hong Kong Polytechnic University, where she was on Dean's List for two academic years. Sherry has shown immerse interest in learning about healthcare and is keen to contribute to healthcare-related topics after studying related fields in her tertiary education.

**Billy S. H. Ho** is Research Assistant at the Hong Kong Institute of Integrative Medicine at The Chinese University of Hong Kong, China. He received his Bachelor of Science (Honors) in Applied Science (Health Studies) with first-class honours from the School of Professional Education and Executive Development (SPEED) of The Hong Kong Polytechnic University. He is Fellow of the Hong Kong College of Community Health Practitioners. He has published in the fields of elderly healthcare and public health issues, including the chapter on "Monitoring Elderly Healthcare and Social Services" in Ageing with Dignity in Hong Kong and Asia – Holistic and Humanistic Care by Springer in 2022.

**Tiffany Cheng Han Leung** is Assistant Professor in the Faculty of Business at the City University of Macau, China. She gained her doctorate from the School of Management at the University of St Andrews (Scotland). Her research interests are environmental, social and governance (ESG), social and environmental accounting (SEA), corporate social responsibility (CSR) and business ethics. She won "Emerald Literati Network Awards for Excellence" in 2017. She was Co-Principal investigator of the Inter-Institutional Development Scheme (IIDS) and a team member of the IIDS and FDS-funded research project in Hong Kong. Tiffany is the coordinator in the Centre for Social and Environmental Accounting Research (CSEAR) North Asia Office in Hong Kong and Macau. Besides, she serves on the Editorial Board of the Social and Environmental Accounting Journal, the board member of the Accounting Forum, and an ad hoc reviewer in a number of accounting and management journals. She also published peer-reviewed articles in journals in management, accounting, and business ethics.

**Ethel S. T. Sha** is a registered social worker at Tung Wah Group of Hospitals. She received her Master of Social Science in Social Work from the Chinese University of Hong Kong and became Senior Addiction Counsellor after working in addiction counselling services for several years. Her interest in health promotion grows while training first-time job seekers to promote health among primary schoolchildren and older adults. She is currently Doctor of Social Science (DSSc) student at the Chinese University of Hong Kong, with a research interest in digital transformation of social services and service management.

**Kelly Jialin Xie** graduated from the Business School of the University of New South Wales. She is currently studying at the City University of Macau as a Doctor of Business Administration (DBA) student and working as an Environmental, Social, and Governance (ESG) consultant with CESGA certification. Her research interests are ESG Governance, ESG Investment, Eco-friendly Products, Gender Equality and Sustainability Development. Her work includes ESG strategy, program implementation, and reporting.

# Foreword

I have the pleasure to write the Foreword for this monograph, *Sustainable Health Promotion Practices and the Global Economy*, led and edited by Dr Ben Fong of the College of Professional and Continuing Education at The Hong Kong Polytechnic University.

Health promotion is an essential and integral activity in primary healthcare for the community. The Hong Kong Government is promoting primary healthcare after the release of the *Primary Healthcare Blueprint* in December 2023. The Primary Healthcare Commission was established in July 2024. Chinese medicine has been serving people in their health and wellness all through the history of China before and after the introduction of Western medicine. Locally, Chinese Medicine Practitioners are providing over 20% of the primary care consultations to the public. Moreover, integrative care is becoming a new trend in primary healthcare and should have much to contribute to promoting health and wellness for individuals, thus supporting the Sustainable Development Goal 3.

Dr Fong's team at the Centre for Ageing and Healthcare Management Research is contributing to the subject of health promotion in the contexts of social determinants, SDGs, the global economy, environmental, ecology, education, and the lifelong framework. I recommend this publication to students, healthcare practitioners, academic colleagues, and the general public.

Lin Zhixiu<br>
Director and Professor of the School of Chinese Medicine<br>
Director of Hong Kong Institute of Integrative Medicine<br>
The Chinese University of Hong Kong<br>
Hong Kong, China

# Foreword

It gives me great pleasure to write the Foreword for this monograph, *Sustainable Health Promotion Practices and the Global Economy*, written by colleagues of the Centre for Ageing and Healthcare Management Research (CAHMR) of the College of Professional and Continuing Education at The Hong Kong Polytechnic University.

Health promotion, as outlined in the 1986 Ottawa Charter, empowers individuals to enhance their control over health, aligning with the universal right to health emphasised in the 2016 Shanghai Declaration by the World Health Organization. This declaration underscores health as an essential resource, a shared social goal, and a political priority globally. The Sustainable Development Goals (SDGs) are identified as instrumental in fostering a duty to invest in health, ensuring universal health coverage, and addressing health inequities. The profound impacts of the COVID-19 pandemic underscore the urgency of strategic investments in responsive healthcare, social support, environmental protection, and resilient systems. The SDGs provide a framework for global health support, presenting both challenges and opportunities for health promotion practices. Recognising health's interconnectedness with various societal aspects, prioritising a robust and adaptable healthcare system becomes imperative in addressing contemporary global challenges.

The dedicated author team, led by Dr Ben Fong, Director of CAHMR, has reviewed post-pandemic practices in health promotion, including first-aid training in education initiatives, addressing the SDGs in the context of social, economic, environmental, and ecological contexts to inform a framework for improved lifelong population health for all. I am confident that this publication will benefit healthcare practitioners, academics, policymakers, students, and the community.

Stephen C. W. Ma, MH, CStJ
Chairman of Medical Services Committee, and
Chairman of Board of Directors (2018–2023)
Sik Sik Yuen
Hong Kong, China

# 1 Health Promotion in the Community – Revisited After COVID-19

*Billy S. H. Ho and Ben Y. F. Fong*

## Introduction

Improving the health of the population in the world and promoting sustainable development have emerged as major goals and challenges of the twenty-first century. Under the dual pressure of rapid population ageing and economic downturn, particularly after the recent pandemic and international wars in some regions, the world is seeking more comprehensive methods to promote a state of complete physical, psychological, emotional, and social health for all people of all ages in an efficient, effective, and sustainable manner. From a micro- and macroeconomic perspective, a healthy population lowers health-care expenses and yields higher long-term returns on investment (Y. Yang et al., 2021; Jack & Lewis, 2009). Several studies and experience have shown that the improvement in public health can result in a significant increase in gross domestic product (GDP), labour productivity, and sustainable economic growth (Raghupathi & Raghupathi, 2020). On the other hand, investing in health has a substantial positive effect on economic growth by mitigating the impact of population ageing (Y. Yang et al., 2021). For global health and continuous economic growth, governments, economists, academics, and health professionals around the world have positively researched and implemented innovative and appropriate health interventions.

Health promotion is one of the major interventions employed in primary care. It is the process of enabling individuals and communities to improve their health and well-being through education and behavioural change. Indeed, the diverse effectiveness of health promotion interventions is described by multiple literature studies in reducing health disparities and advocating health equity. Health promotion has been identified as one of the most important public health activities in sustaining primary health care (PHC). Health promotion enables the creation of a safe foundation and supportive environments for different stakeholders in the community, providing comprehensive information, essential capacities, and opportunities for making conducive and healthy choices (Aadahl et al., 2023). In addition to preventing diseases, and identifying and maintaining the health of people with chronic conditions, health promotion is beneficial in positive public health outcomes and health

DOI: 10.4324/9781032701356-1

equity, and reduction in healthcare expenses (Pati et al., 2017). Besides, health promotion has a positive role in the improvement of life quality, avoidance of premature deaths, and lowering the cost of medical treatment (Kumar & Preetha, 2012).

To respond to the urgent global interconnected challenges and promote sustainable development, United Nations member states have reached a global consensus and commitment to achieve the 2030 Sustainable Development Goals (SDGs), first proposed in 2015. Nonetheless, a significant portion of the global population still lacks access to essential healthcare services as the equitable distribution of the substantial benefits derived from improved longevity and advancements in medical technology have not been fully realised. In many countries, particularly those with low-income economies, notable deficiencies exist in health infrastructure and the capacity to provide essential health services. Indeed, low- and middle-income countries (LMICs) encounter limitations in terms of resources and difficulties in allocating adequate funds towards health promotion and economic development. Challenges remain in achieving the targets of maternal mortality (SDG 3.1), neonatal and child mortality (SDG 3.2), and universal health coverage (UHC) (SDG 3.8) in developing countries. The latest report from the United Nations showed that approximately 800 women worldwide died daily during pregnancy or childbirth in 2020, and 381 million people were pushed into extreme poverty due to the lack of health aid in 2019 (United Nations, 2023). Globally, most LMICs continue to experience high levels of maternal, infant, and neonatal morbidity and mortality, as well as a high number of severe impairments. Approximately 90% of the world's avoidable or treatable visual impairment occurs in developing countries (Haileamlak, 2022). Despite advancements in combating diseases such as HIV and hepatitis (SDG 3.3), marginalised countries, such as sub-Saharan Africa, still bear the greatest burden of communicable diseases (Guégan et al., 2018). Undoubtedly, inadequate healthcare facilities, shortages of health workforce, and limited accessibility to high-quality healthcare are obstacles to the attainment of health-related SDGs.

Furthermore, the Coronavirus Disease 2019 (COVID-19) pandemic and other ongoing public health crises are hampering the progress towards SDG 3 (United Nations, n.d.). Developing countries, already facing socioeconomic challenges, have been disproportionately affected, leading to increased mortality rates among vulnerable populations. Moreover, the decline in economic support and financial resources from developed countries has hindered efforts in developing countries to achieve health for all and the targets of SDG 3. In addition to exacerbating food insecurity, the COVID-19 pandemic has disrupted health services and reduced access to nutrition in most LMICs, posing a significant threat to global health, with higher mortality rates among pregnant women, newborns, and young children being observed during the COVID-19 pandemic (Gajbhiye et al., 2021; Simpson, 2023).

In view of the multifaceted challenges posed by the global spread of the COVID-19 pandemic, this chapter aims to review and analyse the discourse presented in previous global health promotion conferences and the barriers that hinder health promotion practice in achieving SDG 3. Through this analysis, this chapter explores the implications of global health promotion practices at the community level in addressing the complexities of the COVID-19 pandemic and achieving the SDGs.

## Global Health Promotion Charters and Conferences: Progress, Challenges, and Implications

### *The Ottawa Charter for Health Promotion 1986*

The Ottawa Charter made great historical significance in the progress and development of health promotion after the 1978 Alma-Ata Declaration. Back in 1986, the first International Conference on Health Promotion, held in Ottawa, marked a significant milestone in the field of global health. The Ottawa Charter is widely recognised for its broad and holistic view of health promotion, giving a clear and useful framework for health promotion practice. The Ottawa Charter suggested necessary actions to achieve a complete stage of health and put an emphasis on health promotion at the individual level (Capone & Petrillo, 2013). It outlined five crucial components of health promotion actions and preconditions necessary for achieving health. Three basic strategies for health promotion were also established. The Ottawa Charter emphasised organisational involvement and community participation as well as global actions and international cooperation in promoting health from disease diagnosis to prevention. The Ottawa Charter gave a clear definition of health, along with the encouragement of global cooperation on health promotion by improving the social determinants of health. More importantly, the Ottawa Charter illustrated the importance of preventive health behaviours in achieving a complete stage of health rather than just an absence of disease or illness diagnosis. Nonetheless, the Ottawa Charter has been criticised for being overly optimistic and idealistic in addressing the structural and economic determinants of health. The limited consideration for the challenges and barriers to health promotion, particularly some strategies that are difficult to implement in practice in resource-poor settings, hampered long-term sustainable development. To improve the effectiveness of the framework of health promotion programmes, economic goals should be set and promulgated. Specific actions and practices should also be defined and established.

### *The Bangkok Charter for Health Promotion in a Globalised World 2005*

The Bangkok Charter had a specific focus on health promotion strategies and actions which aimed at addressing barriers caused by globalisation (Capone & Petrillo, 2013). Unhealthy lifestyles and the harmful use of alcohol and tobacco persisted in high-income countries at that time, posing challenges to health promotion implementation. The Bangkok Charter elaborated the concept of health promotion as a process of enabling people to increase control over their health and its determinants, leading to the improvement of health (World Health Organization [WHO], 2006). The Bangkok Charter identified essential actions, and commitments needed to address the determinants of health in a globalised world through health promotion, emphasising cooperation and participation within and outside the healthcare settings to achieve health for all. In addition, it highlighted the importance of intersectoral national and local strategies in health promotion. Meanwhile, it also emphasised the potential of health promotion interventions in improving health literacy and empowering individuals to control health determinants and reduce the risks of diseases. Indeed, previous research demonstrated the potential of health promotion interventions in improving health literacy, particularly in educational, occupational, and community settings, thereby empowering individuals to self-control, self-management and the reduction of risk factors (Nutbeam et al., 2021). While criticisms have been raised regarding its handling of power imbalances and economic factors, the Bangkok Charter has further enhanced community participation, engagement, and empowerment, building upon the pivotal concepts introduced in the Ottawa Charter.

### *Helsinki Statement on Health in All Policies 2013*

In 2013, the Helsinki Statement on Health in All Policies (HiAP) was released, highlighting the importance of recognising health as a fundamental human right and in promoting health equity. The statement emphasised the significance of political will and public health policy in promoting health and achieving equity (Regional Office for the Americas of the World Health Organization, n.d.). It acknowledged that unequal political, social, and economic circumstances led to health disparities between and within countries, and Health in All Policies was introduced as a public policy approach to promote health implications across sectors (WHO, 2014). HiAP aims to maximise health benefits and minimise potential harm while addressing social determinants, establishing structures and resources, fostering cross-sector collaboration, building institutional capacity, ensuring transparency and accountability, protecting policies from commercial interests, and involving communities in decision-making and monitoring (Ståhl & Koivusalo, 2021). By embracing the HiAP principles, governments can fulfil their commitments to the United Nations Millennium Development Goals, enhance health promotion effectiveness, ensure effective policy coherence and well-being, and reduce inequalities based on socio-economic status and location.

### *Shanghai Declaration (9th Global Conference on Health Promotion 2016)*

The Shanghai Declaration (WHO, 2016) emphasised the crucial role of good governance, healthy cities, and health literacy as the three fundamental concepts in the implementation and advancement of health promotion practices worldwide. The declaration called for the establishment of universal access to affordable healthcare services and essential health resources through proper regulations, order, and statutes, ensuring the right to health for all. More importantly, the concept of the Shanghai Declaration aligned with the United Nations' 2030 Agenda for 17 SDGs. It urged political action to advance health promotion and the achievement of the SDGs. Some global issues such as climate change, urbanisation, and the increasing prevalence of non-communicable diseases (NCDs) were recognised as essential determinants in the statement. The declaration expanded the traditional scope of health promotion beyond healthy living or NCDs and identified the potential of integrated health promotion measures. It successfully reflected the evolving health promotion standards and the practical challenges. Overall, the Shanghai Declaration highlighted the significance of political commitment and cooperation in promoting health and sustainable development, strengthening the capabilities of nations to address complex and interconnected challenges related to the SDGs (Kickbusch & Nutbeam, 2017).

## Defining Health Promotion Practices: Towards Suitable and Practical Approaches

Having reviewed the major developments in global health promotion as documented in various charters and declarations, it becomes evident that evolving standards, goals, and strategies reflect an increasing recognition of the significance of international cooperation in addressing health challenges. In order to effectively align with the evolving global agenda, this section delves into the theoretical foundations, key principles, and practical applications of health promotion interventions.

Health promotion practices encompass a diverse array of activities and interventions, encompassing a vital and indispensable role in promoting physical health, mental wellness, and social well-being. Nevertheless, the field of health promotion practices has witnessed disparities in its definition across international societies, academia, health professionals, and experts from various disciplines. Initially, health promotion practices were primarily associated with the nursing role, particularly in developing countries, focusing on evidence-based approaches and providing individuals with resources and services to attain their optimal health potential and prevent diseases (Dombrowski et al., 2014). However, some professionals have criticised health promotion for over-focusing on health education and disease prevention (Samson-Akpan et al., 2013). At the community level, effective health promotion practices prioritise the participation and capacity-building of community members or groups, often through empowerment, to address their health needs (Harris & Şandor, 2013). These strategies aim to reduce health inequalities in society in the long term (Vastani & Petrucka, 2016) and drive change at individual, community, national, and global levels (Potvin & Jourdan, 2021). Recent literature highlights the significance of ethical considerations in health promotion practices and emphasises the need for the development of ethical frameworks for health promotion interventions. These frameworks aim to improve health outcomes and promote the well-being of individuals and communities (Blackford et al., 2021). Additionally, health promotion extends to environmental health, which involves addressing environmental factors and the community neighbourhood that can impact health and quality of life (Auld & Hatcher, 2010).

Creating supportive environments that foster complete well-being for individuals is a central commitment of the global health promotion charters and international consensus. Nonetheless, promoting health at the school, community, and workplace levels can be intricate and demanding. Indeed, different stakeholders have different points of view regarding health promotion. Employers focus on improving productivity and reducing absenteeism while schools focus on holistic education. It is important to understand the potential needs and reach a consensus among the various parties. On the other hand, it is crucial for health professionals, governments, and other stakeholders to recognise that there is no universally applicable, flawless approach to health promotion. Instead, the emphasis should be on identifying and implementing health promotion practices that are appropriate and effective within specific contexts. For instance, workplace interventions face constraints such as limited resources, inadequate funding, and the need to establish a culture of health within organisations, which may require a major shift in attitudes, values, and practices while balancing work demands to encourage employer participation and engagement.

This recognition underscores the importance of considering factors such as cultural norms, socioeconomic conditions, and healthcare systems when designing and implementing health promotion initiatives. In the long term, health promotion practices in developing countries should prioritise enhancing water infrastructure, promoting agricultural development, and facilitating nutrition education because food supply and access to clean water are foundational prerequisites for good health in these countries. Notwithstanding, the COVID-19 pandemic has upended the structure of the health promotion model. The traditional healthcare model of disease treatment is not enough to deal with rapidly evolving health needs. Furthermore, the rapidly evolving technology and the globalisation process have intensified the complexity and difficulties in the implementation of health promotion strategies.

Public education is undoubtedly a key element in health promotion and preventive care, but health promotion is a dynamic concept that evolves over time, being shaped by social desires, political will, and public health needs. Previous global health promotion conferences have placed considerable emphasis on the attainment of shared objectives and consensus, as well as the execution of global actions and fostering international cooperation. Consequently, health promotion practices and health-related interventions should prioritise the facilitation of effective communication and collaboration among a broad range of crucial stakeholders, including researchers, practitioners, policymakers, and other key actors. In this context, it becomes increasingly obvious and clear to allow for flexibility in the realignment of priorities within health promotion practices and to adequately respond to the intricate health requirements exhibited by diverse populations across various communities and nations.

## Objective of Sustainable Development Goal 3

From the concept of health promotion practices defined and understood previously, it becomes imperative to situate the practices within the broader framework of global development goals. There is a growing recognition of addressing global challenges, such as sustainable economic growth and environmental issues, which requires the effective implementation of the SDGs. Notably, this understanding is reinforced by each international health promotion conference and the commitment statements, which emphasise the significance of the prerequisites and determinants of health (Raphael, 2013). Globally, the pursuit of global health and the fulfilment of basic health requirements are widely acknowledged as the essential components for advancing towards the SDGs.

The United Nations' Sustainable Development Goal 3 (SDG 3) serves as a pivotal guidepost in this regard. SDG 3 aims to address major health priorities worldwide, including sexual, reproductive, maternal, newborn, child, and adolescent health, communicable and NCDs, UHC, and access to safe, quality, and affordable medicines and vaccines. In a nutshell, SDG 3 seeks to ensure comprehensive well-being and healthy lives for individuals of all ages in all countries (Fong et al., 2021).

## The Relationship Between Global Economy and SDG 3

Lessons from the history and experiences of many countries have shown the correlations between economic development and public health. As suggested by Niu et al. (2021), public health expenditure and financial subsidies tend to increase with the growth of the national economy, which in turn creates substantial synergies in improving the healthcare system and public health policies. Furthermore, economic growth enhances the income and quality of life of the population, resulting in increased attention to better personal health and well-being, living standards, and nutritional status (Alderman et al., 2007). Moreover, improving public health has the potential to reduce the length of sick leave and productivity loss, decrease unemployment rates, and avoid premature retirement, establishing a sound cycle in improving sustainable economic growth (de Oliveira et al., 2023). In addition, economic development can have positive spillover effects on various social determinants of health, such as education, sanitation, and access to clean water. These factors also play a crucial role in improving environmental health (SDG 3.9). In contrast, Hooley et al. (2022) conducted a comprehensive analysis of health insurance data from 100 LMICs and found an average coverage of 31.1% with variations across income groups: 7.9% in low-income countries, 27.3% in LMICs, and 52.5% in upper-middle-income countries. Undoubtedly, countries with low levels of economic development have poor health coverage and limited access to healthcare knowledge and the necessary health services to maintain good health, resulting in poor population health.

Globally, significant progress has been made in tackling the major causes of death and illness, resulting in an increase in life expectancy and a decline in infant and maternal mortality rates since the year 2000. However, the progress made in health outcomes is uneven across and within countries. The least developed countries (LDCs) are characterised as the most vulnerable nations in terms of economic, social, and human development indicators. According to statistics from the United Nations, the 46 LDCs have a combined population of approximately 880 million people, accounting for 12% of the global population (United Nations, n.d.). The average life expectancy at birth in the Organisation for Economic Co-operation and Development (OECD) countries was 80.3 years in 2021, whereas those of South Africa and Indonesia were 65.3 and 68.8 years, respectively (OECD, 2023). This discrepancy reflected the fact that fewer individuals in developing countries lived to older ages, and there were significant health disparities and development inequalities. In addition, LDCs encountered heightened vulnerability to economic shocks and unprecedented pandemics, and they also faced formidable structural obstacles, such as a scarcity of human capital, inadequate infrastructure and healthcare resources, and political instability (United Nations Conference on Trade and Development, 2022). These factors not only contributed to the persistently high poverty rates and malnutrition prevalence but also posed substantial obstacles to the achievement of SDG 3 related to health and well-being. A report from the WHO suggested an additional health investment of 3.9 trillion dollars in 67 countries, made up of 75% of the world's population, would help achieve the health-related SDGs (Stenberg et al., 2017). Negeri (2023) conducted an analysis from 2000 to 2017, focusing on 34 low-income countries, and found that increasing health aid can significantly improve infant mortality rates. It has been estimated that doubling health aid can save the lives of 44 infants per 1,000 live births.

Some studies have highlighted the emergence of nutrition-related chronic diseases in certain developing countries, such as China and Russia, related to the nutrition transition and economic growth. This transition involves shifts in dietary patterns, including increased consumption of red and processed meats, refined grains, and added sugars, which can contribute to the prevalence of chronic diseases, such as cardiovascular disease, obesity, and diabetes (Burggraf et al., 2015). However, economic growth and improvements in healthcare systems can provide significant public health benefits that cannot be easily substituted in contributing better overall health outcomes towards SDG 3. Countries with economic growth have greater resources to invest in healthcare infrastructure, technology, and health promotion, leading to reduced mortality rates, improved access to healthcare services, enhanced disease prevention and control, and increased life expectancy.

## Unprecedented Disruptions: Impacts of COVID-19 on Global Economy and Health Promotion Practices Towards SDG 3

The COVID-19 pandemic has brought about an unparalleled crisis in the global economy. More specifically, its impacts were far-reaching for businesses and financial systems worldwide, causing disruptions in global supply chains, escalating unemployment rates, reducing gross domestic product (GDP), exacerbating poverty, and pushing economies closer to recession (Colombage et al., 2023). Kosycarz (2023) highlights that the repercussions of COVID-19 extend beyond health impacts and have significant ramifications on the overall economy, resulting in challenges related to financing global public goods (GPGs). The economic consequences of the pandemic have had a detrimental impact on public finances and the advancement of SDG 3 priorities, particularly in developing nations, posing additional obstacles to progress (Colombage et al., 2023). Due to the severe global economic recession and domestic fiscal emergencies caused by COVID-19, many donor countries are facing difficult economic situations and are therefore inclined to make deeper cuts in budgetary allocations for humanitarian and medical development assistance (Kim et al., 2023). Unfortunately, LMICs were among the first to experience the brunt of these challenges. In developing countries such as Sri Lanka, the government allocated funds that were originally intended to achieve SDG 3 to address the public health crisis caused by COVID-19. In South Asia, governments had to reallocate healthcare resources to address the significant repercussions of the COVID-19 pandemic, thereby affecting directly or indirectly the continuity and availability of essential child and maternal health services. This resulted in a substantial increase of 228,000 additional child deaths and 11,000 additional maternal deaths in 2020 (United Nations, 2021). In Bangladesh, the pandemic has hindered infrastructure services, leading to high unemployment, high inflation, and other issues, and the progress of a total of 14 SDGs has been seriously affected (Colombage et al., 2023).

Maternal mortality (SDG 3.1) and neonatal and child mortality (SDG 3.2) rates dramatically increased during the pandemic onset, whether in developing countries or developed countries (Simpson, 2023; Wagner et al., 2023). The latest report of the United Nations Children's Fund (UNICEF) demonstrated that approximately 43 countries had failed to meet SDG 3.2 due to limited essential healthcare services and coverage. Although some studies have demonstrated that the influence of COVID-19 on newborns and children had no complications or less severe infected symptoms, the pandemic has undoubtedly reduced women's access to family planning and reproductive healthcare services (Takian et al., 2022). Moreover, in terms of NCDs and mental health (SDG 3.4), the pandemic has delayed or reduced early diagnosis, screening, and treatment of infectious diseases and NCDs such as cancers and cardiovascular disease, resulting in increased morbidity and mortality (Mafham et al., 2020; Takian et al., 2022).

During the COVID-19 pandemic, several countries have demonstrated a lack of preparedness in addressing financial risks and ensuring equitable healthcare access. It was noted that groups with lower socio-economic status tend to have higher health needs but lower healthcare expenditures (Geense et al., 2013). The pandemic has led to a reduction in trade, lower investment flows and disruptions in business activities in developing countries, exacerbating the health inequalities among citizens with lower socio-economic status, especially vulnerable groups such as older people, people with disabilities, and low-income workers (Colombage et al., 2023; Ekanayake & Amirthalingam, 2021; The World Bank, 2022). This is particularly evident from the widespread financial hardships encountered by individuals seeking healthcare services. In certain developed countries like the United States, the combination of substantial medical bills and inadequate insurance coverage has resulted in higher mortality rates among vulnerable groups, directly hindering progress towards UHC (SDG 3.8) (Campbell et al., 2022).

In countries such as Kenya, Colombia, Eswatini, and South Africa, the socio-economic costs associated with COVID-19 infections and deaths among healthcare practitioners (HCPs) were substantial (The World Bank, 2023). These costs included secondary infections and deaths, disrupted essential health services, and decreased productivity. Developing countries, particularly those with low HCP density and staff shortage, were facing the heaviest economic burden due to inadequate personal protective equipment (PPE) and limited essential medical supplies, shortage of human resources, and lack of infection control training (Faure et al., 2022; Mulu et al., 2020). The risk of infection and complications among HCPs was high in developing countries, such as Amhara, Kenya, and certain provinces of South Africa (Mulu et al., 2020; United Nations, 2021). Despite the preventability of HCP infections, LMICs often face insufficient PPE and preventive measures. Consequently, the costs associated with onward viral transmission outweighed those linked to direct HCP infections.

The epidemiologic transition due to urbanisation and lifestyle and globalisation, inadequate healthcare facilities, and insufficient HCPs were the major challenges for maintaining population health in LMICs (Haileamlak, 2022). The COVID-19 pandemic has exacerbated these challenges, leading to increased maternal and neonatal mortality rates, as well as a higher prevalence of communicable and NCDs, limiting LMIC commitments to SDGs. Furthermore, scarce healthcare resources and disruptions in healthcare services have significantly impacted essential healthcare services in many LMICs, resulting in a substantial increase in child and maternal deaths and failure to meet the target of preventable deaths of newborns and children, and most targets of SDG 3.

## Adaptation and Innovation: Reshaping Health Promotion Practices in the Post-COVID-19 Era

The COVID-19 pandemic has drawn global attention to the potential health emergencies and public health crises of the future. Implementation of health promotion strategies, actions, and interventions to achieve SDG 3 is challenging for all nations. These challenges stem from various factors, including financial obstacles, inadequate global collaboration and coordination, limited healthcare personnel, and constrained resources. To achieve the SDGs, it is crucial to implement effective health promotion interventions and strategies.

Learning from past and recent experiences, it is evident that many LMICs will not prioritise measures in addressing health crises until the latter became global matters. LMICs often lack proper infection prevention and control measures, and their healthcare workers are inadequately equipped with knowledge and protective tools (Wang et al., 2020). This not only increases the risk of illness and death for healthcare workers but also disrupts basic healthcare services and causes economic harm. On the other hand, in addition to providing adequate resources and manpower to support health promotion interventions, developed countries can take actions to support the national health of vulnerable countries, including strengthening prevention planning, education, and management in LMICs, researching, developing, and sharing innovative technologies with them (Kim et al., 2023).

Notably, the COVID-19 pandemic highlights the importance of UHC and the need for preparedness. In addition to hospital and institutional settings, community-based and people-centred interventions can provide ongoing support for local, national, and global health promotion. Strengthening health promotion in the community and reforming healthcare systems, as well as focusing on preventive behaviour patterns, not only play a vital role in reducing costs for health and social care systems but also are advantageous in addressing issues stemming from pandemics while promoting global health and economy. Moreover, global actions and international cooperation are the keys to achieving a shared commitment to the SDGs.

## Recommendations

### *Reorientation of International Assistance and Health Aids for Improving Healthcare Systems in Developing Countries*

Significant progress has been observed in the effectiveness of health aids and international investments for improving healthcare systems in developing countries towards SDG 3. However, in low-income countries, approximately 75% of health expenditure is financed by a combination of external medical assistance and inherently regressive out-of-pocket (OOP) expenditures (Adeyi, 2023). From the perspectives of economic stability and distributive justice, OOP payments are not an effective means of healthcare financing. They perpetuate health inequalities and exacerbate issues of resource distribution, leading to a vicious cycle of impoverishment among vulnerable populations (Bayati et al., 2019; Jalali et al., 2021). Moreover, high OOP costs have a significant negative impact on the quality of life, medication compliance, and various health outcomes (Łyszczarz & Abdi, 2021). On the other hand, the COVID-19 pandemic has caused a significant reduction in external health aids in LMICs, highlighting the instability and unsustainability of relying solely on external aids. The OECD has expressed concerns about foreign aids exceeding the government's health expenditure in many LMICs, potentially leading to an overreliance on external aids and lowered policy priorities for healthcare (Adeyi, 2023).

Research has shown that the majority of external aids provided to impoverished countries are directed towards hospital-based treatment services, such as establishing basic medical facilities, funding equipment and medications, training healthcare professionals, and disease treatment. Less emphasis is placed on disease prevention, health promotion, awareness initiatives, and health education (Shajalal et al., 2017). The sustainability of treatment-focused health aids is uncertain and unstable. To achieve long-term development of PHC and SDG 3, governments of various countries should assist LMICs in developing health financing or healthcare insurance systems, rather than relying solely on health donations. This is definitely not a call for developed countries or world organisations to reduce or end health aids, but rather to redirect the funds towards helping developing countries build long-term self-sufficiency and local responsibility by establishing their own resilient infrastructure and sustainable healthcare systems. This could be accompanied by increased investment in global and regional public goods (Jalali et al., 2021; Kodali, 2023). Additionally, strengthening preventive-focused health promotion interventions, healthcare system management, and governance of healthcare, along with the provision of technical assistance, research, education, and the deployment of expert knowledge and evidence-based policy recommendations, would improve the accessibility and affordability of healthcare for impoverished populations and contribute to achieving UHC and SDG 3 (Jalali et al., 2021; Kodali, 2023).

### *Fostering Collaborative Multidisciplinary Approaches in Community Health Promotion After COVID-19*

Considerable literature has shown that the combination of lifestyle practices and positive psychology results in compounding effects, which are beneficial to combat the global mental health crisis. However, these essential elements are often separated in the mental health promotion and primary prevention strategies (Przybylko et al., 2021). Relying solely on the participation of health professionals is insufficient to address the diverse health needs and navigate the potentially complex desires of individuals. Therefore, more health promotion interventions have started involving stakeholders beyond health professionals. These experts may include social workers, clinical psychologists, and teachers, among others. Developing multidisciplinary approaches in community actions is often overlooked when considering culture, sports, and recreation as the health promotion concepts and elements are complex in implementation (Silva et al., 2014). Notably, community sports projects enable the fostering of a sense of belonging, positive self-esteem, and self-efficacy among socially disadvantaged groups through motivational guidance and constructive group dynamics, thereby promoting health and wellness.

In Belgium, health promoters have collaborated with personal trainers to propose low-threshold sports activities targeting the local socially disadvantaged groups and have successfully enhanced the effectiveness of health prevention services (Van der Veken et al., 2020). Similarly, in Australia and New Zealand, researchers analysed and compared the benefits and barriers identified in the literature concerning single health promotion interventions in the community (Mahoney et al., 2021). They developed an online interdisciplinary intervention that integrated dietary modifications, exercise habits, and positive psychology strategies to address the mental health needs of individuals during COVID-19. A significant enhancement in mental well-being and life satisfaction within the interdisciplinary group was noted, as compared to the control groups. In Brazil, some researchers created health interventions and presented them in cultural activities. Although the stakeholders involved were not familiar with the concepts and principles of health promotion, the health promotion elements were applied in relevant areas and successfully improved the community and individual health status, including stimulating the sense of belonging, cultural roots, and community participation (Silva et al., 2014). A study conducted in Israel demonstrated the positive impact of multidisciplinary teams on health outcomes. The joint efforts of professionals from different sectors, such as education, social protection, and the media, resulted in enhanced rates of occult blood tests, blood lipid level control, and influenza vaccination (Schor et al., 2019). In Taiwan, one 20-week-long workplace-based health promotion programme carried out by a multidisciplinary team successfully improved the physical health status and alleviated psychological stress for approximately 300 HCPs (Cheng et al., 2022).

A wealth of research has indicated the important role of multidisciplinary methods as the foundation of community health promotion interventions. In the past, the limited effectiveness of health promotion interventions has been highly attributed to the insufficient involvement of key stakeholders. The international society has gradually recognised that the engagement of a diverse range of experts with various knowledge, qualifications, and skills is conducive to delivering effective health promotion services and achieving the targets outlined in SDG 3. Governments should strengthen the existing multidisciplinary cooperation, communication, and connection to address local and global health needs.

### *Developing Role of Community Health Practitioners in Primary Healthcare*

The COVID-19 pandemic has inflicted profound health and economic consequences, unveiling significant vulnerabilities within global health systems. This has underscored the paramount importance of high-quality PHC during health emergencies. From an economic perspective, enhancing PHC services as public health emergency preparedness (PHEP) can reduce the use of resource-intensive secondary care services and play a key role in promoting overall health outcomes in terms of the health system efficiency and health population equity, thus improving human productivity and economic growth in enhancing resilience and sustainability (Clarke et al., 2021; WHO, 2018). In addition to strengthening the cooperation and coordination between multidiscipline and specialists, governments should develop the important role of community health practitioners (CHPs) in establishing a comprehensive framework for effective improvement in long-term community health promotion (Mittelmark et al., 2017).

CHPs are widely acknowledged as the essential part of maintaining PHC not only improving the local access to essential healthcare services, health education, and health counselling but also playing an indispensable role as the frontline agents to reach community residents, vulnerable groups, and marginalised communities. An international quantitative survey has identified resource constraints as the primary barrier in developing countries (Weiss & Pollack, 2017). These constraints, which encompass limited financial, human, and infrastructural resources, pose significant challenges to the provision of adequate healthcare services in these settings. Nonetheless, it is effective to grant CHPs greater practice authority in primary care consultations, and the long-term results of primary care services can be provided at lower costs and contribute to the sustainability of the healthcare system (Clarke et al., 2021). The return on investment in CHPs is estimated at $10 for every $1 spent in developing countries (WHO, 2018). The contribution of CHPs to the achievement of the SDGs and health outcomes has been demonstrated in high-, middle- and low-income countries (Scott et al., 2018). CHPs enable the availability of essential PHC for the management of NCDs and provision of psychological care and social support, ensuring access to sexual and reproductive health services (Van Iseghem et al., 2023).

### *Empowering Health Promotion in Changing Landscapes: Leveraging Technology for SDG 3 Implementation*

The COVID-19 pandemic has significantly weakened the continuity of the provision of PHC services, leading to the exploration of innovative approaches to health promotion, especially in the field of mental health and emotional wellness. Fortunately, the rapid development of new 5G technology, coupled with the proliferation of internet services and smartphones, has accelerated the adoption of online interventions as a public health promotion strategy. A wealth of studies indicated that online platforms, digital psychotherapy, tele-exercise programmes, and telemedicine have played an effective role in the COVID-19 pandemic, assisting in health promotion, clinical services, and better resource utilisation and reducing the burden on healthcare systems (Chan et al., 2023; B. X. Yang et al., 2021). Indeed, the escalating need for mental health services has effectively been addressed through online interventions during the pandemic. In Mexico and Indonesia, the establishment of online mental health platforms and digital psychotherapy has significantly enhanced public access to mental health professionals, including psychiatrists, psychiatric nurses, and social workers in addressing the growing prevalence of depression and anxiety symptoms (Dominguez-Rodriguez et al., 2022; Geraldina et al., 2023). Besides, in response to the psychological challenges arising from the COVID-19 pandemic, several artificial intelligence (AI) programmes were developed by governments to provide support during the health crises. Notably, in China, a specific AI programme called Tree Holes Rescue was created to monitor individuals who might be at a high risk of suicide, prompting timely intervention when necessary (B. X. Yang et al., 2021). While certain studies have suggested that healthcare professionals may have a preference for face-to-face psychological interventions (Shechter et al., 2020), it is undoubtedly to acknowledge the significant role of online interventions in expanding service options and meeting the increased demand for PHC services (Erku et al., 2023).

On the other hand, telemedicine services showed various benefits in the improvement of preventive health services and quality of life, as well as in lowering healthcare costs and unnecessary administrative expenses. Notably, people with lower socio-economic status are less likely to have medical consultations in the health centre due to a lack of social support and financial subsidies, challenging them to obtain office-based healthcare services (Jezewski et al., 2022). Telemedicine can improve the provision of healthcare and enhance healthcare accessibility for vulnerable groups, communities with limited resources, and patients residing in remote areas, particularly in LMICs (Hoffer-Hawlik et al., 2020). In resource-limited nations such as India, the integration of telemedicine into the healthcare infrastructure has been observed through the implementation of healthcare initiatives, such as the Telemedicine Pilot Project. This project has established a connection between rural hospitals and specialised urban centres, thereby addressing healthcare disparities and fostering improved access to healthcare services (Galagali et al., 2021). Similarly, in the United States of America, an educational telehealth programme has successfully improved the access and usage of telehealth among older adults (Jezewski et al., 2022).

Developed countries have been supporting health promotion initiatives in developing nations by providing data network support, hosting facilities, and software application support. This assistance can help address the changing landscape and challenges of health promotion and will further contribute to a favourable environment for the implementation of SDG 3. By harnessing the power of twenty-first-century information and communication technology, governments, along with civil society, can empower individuals by providing them with health advice and options. This integration enables people to have increased awareness, access, and contact options, thereby transforming these possibilities into tangible realities. Governments and diverse professionals have assimilated the knowledge gained from the COVID-19 pandemic and converted it into novel health promotion practices, encompassing telehealth, remote work arrangements, and online learning (Clarke et al., 2021). These applications of health information and technology (HIT) in delivering PHC services will help to make health promotion more resilient to address the health, economic, and social impacts of pandemic crises and natural disasters. Additionally, international collaboration is imperative in comprehensive research on the acceptability, safety, efficacy, feasibility, and sustainability of teletherapy (Stadler et al., 2023). Language barriers and insufficient digital literacy, as well as internet connection issues, and poor doctor–patient relationships are critical factors that should be addressed (Chung-Lee et al., 2023). In addition, developed countries can assist developing countries in accelerating the incorporation of teletherapy into the professionalisation of PHC by providing digital training and continuing education for relevant personnel, in fulfilling the shared objectives of SDG 3.

### *Advancing Complementary and Alternative Medicine in Community Health Promotion and the Achievement of SDGs*

The global utilisation of complementary and alternative medicine (CAM) is on the rise, with approximately 170 member states of the WHO having incorporated various CAM modalities such as traditional Chinese medicine (TCM), herbal medicine, acupuncture, and indigenous therapies into their healthcare systems (WHO, 2019). CAM is deeply rooted in the historical practices of herbal knowledge and pharmaceutical theories, making it a valuable component in community health promotion aligned with SDG achievements. Within underdeveloped or resource-limited countries, a significant portion of the population heavily relies on traditional herbal medicine as their PHC option (Sen & Chakraborty, 2017). CAM is extensively used by communities and individuals for a wide range of health concerns, including prevention, diagnosis, and treatment of diseases, and managing chronic conditions such as heart diseases, mental illnesses, cancer, and NCDs (Shahjalal et al., 2022). In regions such as Ghana, Saudi Arabia, and Nigeria, herbal medicines are widely used in traditional medical practices, and their potential effectiveness and efficacy in treating diarrhoea and other illnesses are considered by locals to be superior to contemporary medicines (Liheluka et al., 2023a, 2023b). On the other hand, the holistic approach of TCM, which encompasses herbal medicine, is extensively employed in several Asian countries for various conditions. In Taiwan, TCM has exhibited notable benefits in enhancing the survival rates of patients diagnosed with conditions such as multiple myeloma (Huang et al., 2020). Moreover, TCM has been applied in the management of diverse ailments, encompassing musculoskeletal disorders, chronic obstructive pulmonary disease, and various types of cancers (Huang et al., 2020; Li et al., 2021; Liang et al., 2020; Liu et al., 2021; Wang et al., 2021). Additionally, several studies have highlighted the potential of TCM in anti-ageing treatments and the management of multiple neurodegenerative diseases, such as Alzheimer's disease and Parkinson's disease, thus underscoring the multifaceted applications of TCM (Du et al., 2023; Zhang et al., 2019).

From an economic standpoint, CAM serves as an accessible and relatively cost-effective alternative for disease management. For both developed countries and developing countries, the public can receive CAM at an affordable price to promote individual health in the PHC setting (Tangkiatkumjai et al., 2020). Some LMICs with limited UHC, such as rural areas of South Africa and Nepal, commonly utilise CAM for the management of non-communicable and chronic diseases, including cancers, cardiovascular disease, diabetes, joint pain, heart disease, hypertension, rheumatoid arthritis, stroke, and other ailments (Hughes et al., 2022; Kunwar et al., 2010). Despite the recognition of the increasing value of traditional medicine in the Shanghai Declaration, investment in the development of CAM still remains limited. The effectiveness and efficacy of CAM have often been underestimated in the past. However, there is a growing acknowledgement and appreciation of CAM's role in enhancing community health. Increasing studies have also investigated knowledge, attitude, utilisation, acceptance, and satisfaction of different CAM modalities such as Chinese medicine (Ng et al., 2022). By integrating and expanding the availability of CAM, within the framework of PHC, individuals can benefit from a comprehensive and accessible healthcare system. This integration aims to ensure that CAM practices are easily accessible and provided at the PHC level, thereby contributing to the delivery of holistic and patient-centred care (WHO, 2019).

Furthermore, research and empirical evidence are crucial to determine the efficacy, safety, and quality of CAM, including its integration into PHC and UHC. Comprehensive and rigorous investigations into the effectiveness and impact of CAM interventions are needed to inform evidence-based decision-making and optimise healthcare outcomes (WHO, 2019). To ensure the safety and quality of herbal medicines and supplement products, it is imperative to strengthen the monitoring efforts of relevant regulatory agencies and implement regular quality testing and production standards, ensuring that only safe and high-quality herbal medicines and supplements reach the market (Ekor, 2014). Additionally, botanists, phytochemists, pharmacologists, and healthcare professionals should strengthen the collaboration in conducting robust research on potential adverse reactions, associated risks, contraindications, and interactions with conventional drugs because it is crucial in safeguarding population health.

In the long term, the international society should explore ways to help CAM-related practitioners such as Chinese medicine practitioners (CMPs) to construct professional identities in licensing and institutionalisation of training (Chiu & Sze, 2021). In addition, governments should provide training to orthodox healthcare professionals such as doctors, nurses, all health professionals, and pharmacists on the use and interactions of herbal medicines, to protect public health and promote the safe and rational use of medicine (Ekor, 2014). Policymakers, healthcare professionals, community members, and stakeholders must redefine the role of CAM in the healthcare system, particularly health promotion, to advance UHC and contribute to the SDGs, promoting the overall well-being of individuals.

## Conclusion

The challenges faced by both developed and developing countries in achieving SDG 3 are complex and interconnected. Many health experts, policymakers, and civil society leaders have emphasised the need for comprehensive strategies and international collaboration to address the barriers to SDG 3 implementation. The COVID-19 pandemic has significantly undermined progress made towards SDG 3, highlighting the importance of strengthening international cooperation and resource sharing to mitigate the negative impacts of the current public health crisis and future global uncertainties. Additionally, expediting the development of resilient health systems is crucial in the preparedness and effective management of future health crises. There is still much work to be done to address various health disparities and inequalities worldwide. By continuously enhancing oversight and regulation in these areas, together with strong health promotion in the community, healthcare systems can strive to achieve SDG 3 by providing accessible, equitable, and high-quality healthcare services to populations worldwide.

## References

Aadahl, M., Vardinghus-Nielsen, H., Bloch, P., Jørgensen, T. S., Pisinger, C., Tørslev, M. K., Klinker, C. D., Birch, S. D., Bøggild, H., & Toft, U. (2023). Our healthy community conceptual framework and intervention model for health promotion and disease prevention in municipalities. *International Journal of Environmental Research and Public Health*, *20*(5), 3901. https://doi.org/10.3390/ijerph20053901

Adeyi, O. (2023). In focus: Transitioning out of aid dependency in health. In *Development co-operation report 2023: Debating the aid system*. OECD Publishing. https://doi.org/10.1787/2c087f8b-en

Alderman, H., Behrman, J. R., & Hoddinott, J. (2007). Economic and nutritional analyses offer substantial synergies for understanding human nutrition. *The Journal of Nutrition*, *137*(3), 537–544. https://doi.org/10.1093/jn/137.3.537

Auld, M. E., & Hatcher, M. T. (2010). Environmental health promotion: Advancing the science and practice. *Health Promotion Practice*, *11*(3), 301–302. https://doi.org/10.1177/1524839910364371

Bayati, M., Mehrolhassani, M. H., & Yazdi-Feyzabadi, V. (2019). A paradoxical situation in regressivity or progressivity of out of pocket payment for health care: Which one is a matter of the health policy maker's decision to intervention? *Cost Effectiveness & Resource*, *17*, 28. https://doi.org/10.1186/s12962-019-0197-0

Blackford, K., Leavy, J. E., Vidler, A. C., Chamberlain, D., Pollard, C., Riley, T., Milligan, M., & Jancey, J. (2021). Initiatives and partnerships in an Australian metropolitan obesity prevention system: A social network analysis. *BMC Public Health*, *21*(1), 1542. https://doi.org/10.1186/s12889-021-11599-7

Burggraf, C., Kuhn, L., Zhao, Q. R., Teuber, R., & Glauben, T. (2015). Economic growth and nutrition transition: An empirical analysis comparing demand elasticities for foods in China and Russia. *Journal of Integrative Agriculture*, *14*(6), 1008–1022.

Campbell, T., Galvani, A. P., Friedman, G., & Fitzpatrick, M. C. (2022). Exacerbation of COVID-19 mortality by the fragmented United States healthcare system: A retrospective observational study. *Lancet Regional Health. Americas*, *12*, 100264. https://doi.org/10.1016/j.lana.2022.100264

Capone, V., & Petrillo, G. (2013). Health promotion in international documents: Strengths and weaknesses from the perspective of community empowerment. *Journal of Community & Applied Social Psychology*, *23*(2), 98–114. https://doi.org/10.1002/casp.2103

Chan, K. O. W., Yuen, P. P., Fong, B. Y. F., Law, V. T. S., Ng, F. S. F., Fung, W. C. P., Ng, T. K. C., & Cheung, I. S. (2023). Effectiveness of telehealth in preventive care: A study protocol for a randomised controlled trial of tele-exercise programme involving older people with possible sarcopenia or at risk of fall. *BMC Geriatrics*, *23*, 845. https://doi.org/10.1186/s12877-023-04535-4

Cheng, K. H., Wu, N. K., Chen, C. T., Hsu, C. Y., Lin, Y. A., Luo, J. J., Lee, L. A., & Chuang, H. H. (2022). Effectiveness and response differences of a multidisciplinary workplace health promotion program for healthcare workers. *Frontiers in Medicine*, *9*, 930165. https://doi.org/10.3389/fmed.2022.930165

Chiu, S. W., & Sze, T. O. (2021). Revival or innovation? Chinese medicine at the crossroads of professionalization in Hong Kong. *SSM-Qualitative Research in Health*, *1*, 100004. https://doi.org/10.1016/j.ssmqr.2021.100004

Chung-Lee, L., Catallo, C., & Meade, A. (2023). What are COVID-19 patient preferences for and experiences with virtual care? Findings from a scoping review. *Journal of Patient Experience*, *10*, 23743735231215603. https://doi.org/10.1177/23743735231215603

Clarke, L., Anderson, M., Anderson, R., Klausen, M. B., Forman, R., Kerns, J., Rabe, A., Kristensen, S. R., Theodorakis, P., Valderas, J., Kluge, H., & Mossialos, E. (2021). Economic aspects of delivering primary care services: An evidence synthesis to inform policy and research priorities. *The Milbank Quarterly*, *99*(4), 974–1023. https://doi.org/10.1111/1468-0009.12536

Colombage, S. R. N., Barua, S., Nanayakkara, M., & Colombage, U. N. (2023). COVID-19 effects on public finance and SDG priorities in developing countries: Comparative evidence from Bangladesh and Sri Lanka. *The European Journal of Development Research*, *35*(1), 85–111. https://doi.org/10.1057/s41287-022-00558-6

de Oliveira, C., Saka, M., Bone, L., & Jacobs, R. (2023). The role of mental health on workplace productivity: A critical review of the literature. *Applied Health Economics and Health Policy*, *21*(2), 167–193. https://doi.org/10.1007/s40258-022-00761-w

Dombrowski, S. U., Knittle, K., Avenell, A., Araújo-Soares, V., & Sniehotta, F. F. (2014). Long term maintenance of weight loss with non-surgical interventions in obese adults: Systematic review and meta-analyses of randomised controlled trials. *BMJ (Clinical Research Ed.)*, *348*, g2646. https://doi.org/10.1136/bmj.g2646

Dominguez-Rodriguez, A., Martínez-Arriaga, R. J., Herdoiza-Arroyo, P. E., Bautista-Valerio, E., de la Rosa-Gómez, A., Castellanos Vargas, R. O., Lacomba-Trejo, L., Mateu-Mollá, J., Lupercio Ramírez, M. J., Figueroa González, J. A., & Ramírez Martínez, F. R. (2022). E-health psychological intervention for COVID-19 healthcare workers: Protocol for its implementation and evaluation. *International Journal of Environmental Research and Public Health*, *19*(19), 12749. https://doi.org/10.3390/ijerph191912749

Du, X., Lou, N., Hu, S., Xiao, R., Chu, C., Huang, Q., Lu, L., Li, S., & Yang, J. (2023). Anti-aging of the nervous system and related neurodegenerative diseases with Chinese herbal medicine. *American Journal of Alzheimer's Disease & Other Dementias*, *38*, 15333175231205445. https://doi.org/10.1177/15333175231205445

Ekanayake, A., & Amirthalingam, K. (2021). The economic impact of the Covid-19 pandemic on Sri Lankan migrants in Qatar. *Comparative Migration Studies*, *9*(1), 38. https://doi.org/10.1186/s40878-021-00246-0

Ekor, M. (2014). The growing use of herbal medicines: Issues relating to adverse reactions and challenges in monitoring safety. *Frontiers in Pharmacology*, *4*, 177. https://doi.org/10.3389/fphar.2013.00177

Erku, D., Khatri, R., Endalamaw, A., Wolka, E., Nigatu, F., Zewdie, A., & Assefa, Y. (2023). Digital health interventions to improve access to and quality of primary health care services: A scoping review. *International Journal of Environmental Research and Public Health*, *20*(19), 6854. https://doi.org/10.3390/ijerph20196854

Faure, J. A., Wang, C. W., Chen, C. S., & Chan, C. C. (2022). Assessment of the functional capacity and preparedness of the Haitian healthcare system to fight against the

COVID-19 pandemic: A narrative review. *Healthcare (Basel, Switzerland)*, *10*(8), 1428. https://doi.org/10.3390/healthcare10081428

Fong, B. Y. F., Law, V. T. S., Leung, T. C. H., Lo, M. F., Ng, T. K. C., & Yee, H. H. L. (2021). *Sustainable development goal 3 – Health and well-being of ageing in Hong Kong*. Routledge.

Gajbhiye, R. K., Sawant, M. S., Kuppusamy, P., Surve, S., Pasi, A., Prusty, R. K., Mahale, S. D., & Modi, D. N. (2021). Differential impact of COVID-19 in pregnant women from high-income countries and low- to middle-income countries: A systematic review and meta-analysis. *International Journal of Gynecology & Obstetrics*, *155*(1), 48–56. https://doi.org/10.1002/ijgo.13793

Galagali, P. M., Ghosh, S., & Bhargav, H. (2021). The role of telemedicine in child and adolescent healthcare in India. *Current Pediatrics Reports*, *9*(4), 154–161. https://doi.org/10.1007/s40124-021-00253-w

Geense, W. W., van de Glind, I. M., Visscher, T. L., & van Achterberg, T. (2013). Barriers, facilitators and attitudes influencing health promotion activities in general practice: An explorative pilot study. *BMC Family Practice*, *14*, 20. https://doi.org/10.1186/1471-2296-14-20

Geraldina, A. M., Suen, M. W., & Suanrueang, P. (2023). Online mental health services during COVID-19 pandemic in Indonesia: Challenges from psychologist perspective. *PLoS ONE*, *18*(6), e0285490. https://doi.org/10.1371/journal.pone.0285490

Guégan, J. F., Suzán, G., Kati-Coulibaly, S., Bonpamgue, D. N., & Moatti, J. P. (2018). Sustainable Development Goal# 3, "health and well-being", and the need for more integrative thinking. *Veterinaria México OA*, *5*(2). https://doi.org/10.21753/vmoa.5.2.443

Haileamlak, A. (2022). The impact of COVID-19 on non-communicable diseases. *Ethiopian Journal of Health Sciences*, *32*(1), 1–2. https://doi.org/10.4314/ejhs.v32i1.1

Harris, N., & Sandor, M. (2013). Defining sustainable practice in community-based health promotion: A Delphi study of practitioner perspectives. *Health Promotion Journal of Australia*, *24*(1), 53–60. https://doi.org/10.1071/HE12908

Hoffer-Hawlik, M. A., Moran, A. E., Burka, D., Kaur, P., Cai, J., Frieden, T. R., & Gupta, R. (2020). Leveraging telemedicine for chronic disease management in low- and middle-income countries during Covid-19. *Global Heart*, *15*(1), 63. https://doi.org/10.5334/gh.852

Hooley, B., Afriyie, D. O., Fink, G., & Tediosi, F. (2022). Health insurance coverage in low-income and middle-income countries: Progress made to date and related changes in private and public health expenditure. *BMJ Global Health*, *7*(5), e008722. https://doi.org/10.1136/bmjgh-2022-008722

Huang, C. Y., Wu, M. Y., Kuo, Y. H., Tou, S. I., & Yen, H. R. (2020). Chinese herbal medicine is helpful for survival improvement in patients with multiple myeloma in Taiwan: A nationwide retrospective matched-cohort study. *Integrative Cancer Therapies*, *19*, 1534735420943280. https://doi.org/10.1177/1534735420943280

Hughes, G. D., Aboyade, O. M., Okonji, O. C., Clark, B., Bawa, W. A., Xavier, C., & Rasu, R. S. (2022). Cost of traditional herbal medicines for noncommunicable diseases in rural and urban communities in South Africa. *Value in Health Regional Issues*, *29*, 66–75. https://doi.org/10.1016/j.vhri.2021.08.006

Jack, W., & Lewis, M. (2009). *Health investments and economic growth: Macroeconomic evidence and microeconomic foundations*. World Bank.

Jalali, F. S., Bikineh, P., & Delavari, S. (2021). Strategies for reducing out of pocket payments in the health system: A scoping review. *Cost Effectiveness and Resource*, *19*(1), 47. https://doi.org/10.1186/s12962-021-00301-8

Jezewski, E., Miller, A., Eusebio, M., & Potter, J. (2022). Targeted telehealth education increases interest in using telehealth among a diverse group of low-income older adults. *International Journal of Environmental Research and Public Health*, *19*(20), 13349. https://doi.org/10.3390/ijerph192013349

Kickbusch, I., & Nutbeam, D. (2017). A watershed for health promotion. *Health Promotion International*, *32*(1), 2–6. https://doi.org/10.1093/heapro/daw112

Kim, Y., Lee, S. H., & Cho, Y. J. (2023). Donor motivation in the era of the COVID-19 crisis: Focusing on South Korean health diplomacy and response aid to COVID-19. *International Area Studies Review*, *26*(1), 71–86. https://doi.org/10.1177/22338659231151409

Kodali, P. B. (2023). Achieving universal health coverage in low- and middle-income countries: Challenges for policy post-pandemic and beyond. *Risk Management and Healthcare Policy*, *16*, 607–621. https://doi.org/10.2147/RMHP.S366759

Kosycarz, E. (2023). Governing global health by international organizations amid the global challenges of today, and its impact on sustainable development. In *Global public goods and sustainable development in the practice of international organizations* (pp. 274–300). Brill.

Kumar, S., & Preetha, G. (2012). Health promotion: An effective tool for global health. *Indian Journal of Community Medicine: Official Publication of Indian Association of Preventive & Social Medicine*, *37*(1), 5–12. https://doi.org/10.4103/0970-0218.94009

Kunwar, R. M., Shrestha, K. P., & Bussmann, R. W. (2010). Traditional herbal medicine in far-west Nepal: A pharmacological appraisal. *Journal of Ethnobiology and Ethnomedicine*, *6*, 35. https://doi.org/10.1186/1746-4269-6-35

Li, H., Wu, R., Yu, H., Zheng, Q., & Chen, Y. (2021). Bioactive herbal extracts of traditional Chinese medicine applied with the biomaterials: For the current applications and advances in the musculoskeletal system. *Frontiers in Pharmacology*, *12*, 778041. https://doi.org/10.3389/fphar.2021.778041

Liang, Q., Zhang, K., Wang, S., Xu, X., Liu, Y., Cui, S., & Liu, L. (2020). Acupuncture for cancer pain – An adjuvant therapy for cancer pain relief. *The American Journal of Chinese Medicine*, *48*(8), 1769–1786. https://doi.org/10.1142/S0192415X20500883

Liheluka, E., Gibore, N. S., Lusingu, J. P. A., Gesase, S., Minja, D. T. R., Lamshöft, M., Dekker, D., & Bali, T. (2023a). Medicinal plants for treatment of diarrhoeal diseases among under-five children: Experience from traditional healers in north-eastern Tanzania. *BMC Complementary Medicine and Therapies*, *23*(1), 379. https://doi.org/10.1186/s12906-023-04216-0

Liheluka, E., Gibore, N. S., Lusingu, J. P. A., Liheluka, E., Gibore, N. S., Lusingu, J. P., Gesase, S., Minja, D. T. R., Lamshöft, M., Dekker, D., & Bali, T. (2023b). Community perceptions on the effectiveness of herbal medicines and factors associated with their use in managing diarrhoea among under-five children in north-eastern Tanzania. *Tropical Medicine and Health*, *51*(48). https://doi.org/10.1186/s41182-023-00537-5

Liu, S., Lai, J., Wu, L., & Guo, X. (2021). Chinese medicine for chronic obstructive pulmonary disease: A pilot study on patient preferences. *Patient Preference and Adherence*, *15*, 1529–1535. https://doi.org/10.2147/PPA.S316872

Łyszczarz, B., & Abdi, Z. (2021). Factors associated with out-of-pocket health expenditure in polish regions. *Healthcare (Basel, Switzerland)*, *9*(12), 1750. https://doi.org/10.3390/healthcare9121750

Mafham, M. M., Spata, E., Goldacre, R., Gair, D., Curnow, P., Bray, M., Hollings, S., Roebuck, C., Gale, C. P., Mamas, M. A., Deanfield, J. E., de Belder, M. A., Luescher, T. F., Denwood, T., Landray, M. J., Emberson, J. R., Collins, R., Morris, E. J. A., Casadei, B., & Baigent, C. (2020). COVID-19 pandemic and admission rates for and management of acute coronary syndromes in England. *Lancet (London, England)*, *396*(10248), 381–389. https://doi.org/10.1016/S0140-6736(20)31356-8

Mahoney, A. E. J., Elders, A., Li, I., David, C., Haskelberg, H., Guiney, H., & Millard, M. (2021). A tale of two countries: Increased uptake of digital mental health services during the COVID-19 pandemic in Australia and New Zealand. *Internet Interventions*, *25*, 100439. https://doi.org/10.1016/j.invent.2021.100439

Mittelmark, M. B., Sagy, S., Eriksson, M., Bauer, G. F., Pelikan, J. M., Lindström, B., & Espnes, G. A. (Eds.). (2017). *The handbook of salutogenesis*. Springer.

Mulu, G. B., Kebede, W. M., Worku, S. A., Mittiku, Y. M., & Ayelign, B. (2020). Preparedness and responses of healthcare providers to combat the spread of COVID-19 among North Shewa Zone Hospitals, Amhara, Ethiopia, 2020. *Infection and Drug Resistance*, *13*, 3171–3178. https://doi.org/10.2147/IDR.S265829

Negeri, K. G. (2023). The long-run effects of health aid in low-income countries. *Journal of Public Health in Africa*, *14*(4), 2219. https://doi.org/10.4081/jphia.2023.2219

Ng, T. K., Lo, M. F., & Fong, B. Y. (2022). Knowledge, attitude, utilisation and satisfaction of traditional Chinese medicine in Hong Kong. *International Journal of Pharmaceutical and Healthcare Marketing*, *16*(1), 123–137. https://doi.org/10.1108/IJPHM-08-2020-0068

Niu, X. T., Yang, Y. C., & Wang, Y. C. (2021). Does the economic growth improve public health? A cross-regional heterogeneous study in China. *Frontiers in Public Health*, *9*, 704155. https://doi.org/10.3389/fpubh.2021.704155

Nutbeam, D., Corbin, J. H., & Lin, V. (2021). The continuing evolution of health promotion. *Health Promotion International*, *36*(Supplement_1), i1–i3. https://doi.org/10.1093/heapro/daab150

OECD. (2023). *Health at a glance 2023: OECD indicators*. OECD Publishing. https://doi.org/10.1787/7a7afb35-en

Pati, S., Chauhan, A. S., Mahapatra, S., Sinha, R., & Pati, S. (2017). Practicing health promotion in primary care -a reflective enquiry. *Journal of Preventive Medicine and Hygiene*, *58*(4), E288–E293. https://doi.org/10.15167/2421-4248/jpmh2017.58.4.749

Potvin, L., & Jourdan, D. (2021). Health promotion research has come of age! Structuring the field based on the practices of health promotion researchers. *Global Health Promotion*, *28*(4), 26–35. https://doi.org/10.1177/17579759211044077

Przybylko, G., Morton, D., Kent, L., Morton, J., Hinze, J., Beamish, P., & Renfrew, M. (2021). The effectiveness of an online interdisciplinary intervention for mental health promotion: A randomized controlled trial. *BMC Psychology*, *9*(1), 77. https://doi.org/10.1186/s40359-021-00577-8

Raghupathi, V., & Raghupathi, W. (2020). Healthcare expenditure and economic performance: Insights from the United States data. *Frontiers in Public Health*, *8*, 156. https://doi.org/10.3389/fpubh.2020.00156

Raphael, D. (2013). The political economy of health promotion: Part 2, national provision of the prerequisites of health. *Health Promotion International*, *28*(1), 112–132. https://doi.org/10.1093/heapro/dar058

Regional Office for the Americas of the World Health Organization. (n.d.). *Health in all policies*. www.paho.org/en/topics/health-all-policies

Samson-Akpan, E., Edet, O. B., Akpabio, I. I., & Asuquo, E. (2013). Perceived relative factors influencing nurses' practice of health promotion for women in Calabar, Cross River State, Nigeria. *International Journal of Nursing and Midwifery*, *5*(3), 46. https://ecommons.aku.edu/cgi/viewcontent.cgi?article=1226&context=eastafrica_fhs_sonam

Schor, A., Bergovoy-Yellin, L., Landsberger, D., Kolobov, T., & Baron-Epel, O. (2019). Multidisciplinary work promotes preventive medicine and health education in primary care: A cross-sectional survey. *Israel Journal of Health Policy Research*, *8*(1), 50. https://doi.org/10.1186/s13584-019-0318-4

Scott, K., Beckham, S. W., Gross, M., Pariyo, G., Rao, K. D., Cometto, G., & Perry, H. B. (2018). What do we know about community-based health worker programs? A systematic review of existing reviews on community health workers. *Human Resources for Health*, *16*(1), 39. https://doi.org/10.1186/s12960-018-0304-x

Sen, S., & Chakraborty, R. (2017). Revival, modernization and integration of Indian traditional herbal medicine in clinical practice: Importance, challenges and future. *Journal of Traditional and Complementary Medicine*, *7*(2), 234–244. https://doi.org/10.1016/j.jtcme.2016.05.006

Shahjalal, M., Chakma, S. K., Ahmed, T., Yasmin, I., Mahumud, R. A., & Hossain, A. (2022). Prevalence and determinants of using complementary and alternative medicine for the treatment of chronic illnesses: A multicenter study in Bangladesh. *PLoS ONE*, *17*(1), e0262221. https://doi.org/10.1371/journal.pone.0262221

Shajalal, M., Xu, J., Jing, J., King, M., Zhang, J., Wang, P., Bouey, J., & Cheng, F. (2017). China's engagement with development assistance for health in Africa. *Global Health Research and Policy*, *2*, 24. https://doi.org/10.1186/s41256-017-0045-8

Shechter, A., Diaz, F., Moise, N., Anstey, D. E., Ye, S., Agarwal, S., Birk, J. L., Brodie, D., Cannone, D. E., Chang, B., Claassen, J., Cornelius, T., Derby, L., Dong, M., Givens, R. C., Hochman, B., Homma, S., Kronish, I. M., Lee, S. A. J., . . . & Abdalla, M. (2020). Psychological distress, coping behaviors, and preferences for support among New York healthcare workers during the COVID-19 pandemic. *General Hospital Psychiatry*, *66*, 1–8. https://doi.org/10.1016/j.genhosppsych.2020.06.007

Silva, K. L., Sena, R. R., Belga, S. M., Silva, P. M., & Rodrigues, A. T. (2014). Promoção da saúde: Desafios revelados em práticas exitosas [Health promotion: Challenges revealed in successful practices]. *Revista de Saude Publica*, *48*(1), 76–85. https://doi.org/10.1590/s0034-8910.2014048004596

Simpson, K. R. (2023). Effect of the COVID-19 pandemic on maternal health in the United States. *MCN. The American Journal of Maternal Child Nursing*, *48*(2), 61. https://doi.org/10.1097/NMC.0000000000000895

Stadler, M., Jesser, A., Humer, E., Haid, B., Stippl, P., Schimböck, W., Maaß, E., Schwanzar, H., Leithner, D., Pieh, C., & Probst, T. (2023). Remote psychotherapy during the COVID-19 pandemic: A mixed-methods study on the changes experienced by Austrian psychotherapists. *Life (Basel, Switzerland)*, *13*(2), 360. https://doi.org/10.3390/life13020360

Ståhl, T., & Koivusalo, M. (2021). Health in all policies: Concept, purpose, and implementation. In I. Kickbusch, D. Ganten & M. Moeti (Eds.), *Handbook of global health*. Springer. https://doi.org/10.1007/978-3-030-45009-0_80

Stenberg, K., Hanssen, O., Edejer, T. T., Bertram, M., Brindley, C., Meshreky, A., Rosen, J. E., Stover, J., Verboom, P., Sanders, R., & Soucat, A. (2017). Financing transformative health systems towards achievement of the health Sustainable Development Goals: A model for projected resource needs in 67 low-income and middle-income countries. *The Lancet Global Health*, *5*(9), e875–e887. https://doi.org/10.1016/S2214-109X(17)30263-2

Takian, A., Raoofi, A., & Haghighi, H. (2022). COVID-19 pandemic: The fears and hopes for SDG 3, with focus on prevention and control of noncommunicable diseases (SDG 3.4) and universal health coverage (SDG 3.8). *COVID-19 and the Sustainable Development Goals*, 211–234. https://doi.org/10.1016/B978-0-323-91307-2.00014-6

Tangkiatkumjai, M., Boardman, H., & Walker, D. M. (2020). Potential factors that influence usage of complementary and alternative medicine worldwide: A systematic review. *BMC Complementary Medicine and Therapies*, *20*(1), 363. https://doi.org/10.1186/s12906-020-03157-2

United Nations. (2021). *The sustainable development goals report 2021*. https://unstats.un.org/sdgs/report/2021/The-Sustainable-Development-Goals-Report-2021.pdf

United Nations. (2023). *The sustainable development goals report 2023: Special edition towards a rescue plan for people and planet*. https://unstats.un.org/sdgs/report/2023/The-Sustainable-Development-Goals-Report-2023.pdf

United Nations. (n.d.). *Goal 3: Ensure healthy lives and promote well-being for all at all ages*. www.un.org/sustainabledevelopment/health/

United Nations Conference on Trade and Development. (2022, April 4). *Four key challenges facing least developed countries*. https://unctad.org/news/four-key-challenges-facing-least-developed-countries

Van der Veken, K., Lauwerier, E., & Willems, S. J. (2020). How community sport programs may improve the health of vulnerable population groups: A program theory. *International Journal for Equity in Health*, *19*(1), 74. https://doi.org/10.1186/s12939-020-01177-5

Van Iseghem, T., Jacobs, I., Vanden Bossche, D., Delobelle, P., Willems, S., Masquillier, C., & Decat, P. (2023). The role of community health workers in primary healthcare in the WHO-EU region: A scoping review. *International Journal for Equity in Health*, *22*(1), 134. https://doi.org/10.1186/s12939-023-01944-0

Vastani, M., & Petrucka, P. M. (2016). Integration of health promotion into nursing practice: A case study in Pakistan. *Open Journal of Nursing*, *6*(1), 37. https://ecommons.aku.edu/pakistan_fhs_son/157

Wagner, Z., Heft-Neal, S., Wang, Z., Jing, R., & Bendavid, E. (2023). Infant and neonatal mortality during the Covid-19 pandemic: An interrupted time series analysis from five low- and middle-income countries. *medRxiv: The Preprint Server for Health Sciences*. https://doi.org/10.1101/2023.08.03.23293619

Wang, C., Lin, K. Y., Wu, M. Y., Lin, C. L., Lin, J. G., Chang, C. Y., Lin, W. C., & Yen, H. R. (2021). Adjunctive Chinese herbal medicine treatment is associated with an improved survival rate in patients with cervical cancer in Taiwan: A matched cohort study. *Integrative Cancer Therapies*, *20*, 15347354211061752. https://doi.org/10.1177/15347354211061752

Wang, H., Cleary, P. D., Little, J., & Auffray, C. (2020). Communicating in a public health crisis. *The Lancet. Digital Health*, *2*(10), e503. https://doi.org/10.1016/S2589-7500(20)30197-7

Weiss, B., & Pollack, A. A. (2017). Barriers to global health development: An international quantitative survey. *PLoS ONE*, *12*(10), e0184846. https://doi.org/10.1371/journal.pone.0184846

The World Bank. (2022, October 6). *The World Bank in Sri Lanka*. www.worldbank.org/en/country/srilanka/overview

The World Bank. (2023, July 26). *The economic burden of COVID-19 infections amongst health care workers*. www.worldbank.org/en/topic/health/publication/economic-cost-covid-health-care-workers

World Health Organization. (2006). The Bangkok Charter for health promotion in a globalized world. *Health Promotion International*, *21*(suppl_1), 10–14. https://doi.org/10.1093/heapro/dal046

World Health Organization. (2014, April 23). *Health in all policies: Helsinki statement. Framework for country action*. www.who.int/publications/i/item/9789241506908

World Health Organization. (2016, November 21). *Shanghai declaration on promoting health in the 2030 agenda for sustainable development*. https://iris.who.int/bitstream/handle/10665/259183/WHO-NMH-PND-17.5-eng.pdf?sequence=1

World Health Organization. (2018, May 8). *Building the economic case for primary health care: A scoping review*. www.who.int/publications/i/item/WHO-HIS-SDS-2018.48

World Health Organization. (2019, June 4). *WHO global report on traditional and complementary medicine 2019*. www.who.int/publications/i/item/978924151536

Yang, B. X., Xia, L., Liu, L., Nie, W., Liu, Q., Li, X. Y., Ao, M. Q., Wang, X. Q., Xie, Y. D., Liu, Z., Huang, Y. J., Huang, Z., Gong, X., & Luo, D. (2021). A suicide monitoring and crisis intervention strategy based on knowledge graph technology for "tree hole" microblog users in China. *Frontiers in Psychology*, *12*, 674481. https://doi.org/10.3389/fpsyg.2021.674481

Yang, Y., Zheng, R., & Zhao, L. (2021). Population aging, health investment and economic growth: Based on a cross-country panel data analysis. *International Journal of Environmental Research and Public Health*, *18*(4), 1801. https://doi.org/10.3390/ijerph18041801

Zhang, Z., Zhang, S., Lui, C. N. P., Zhu, P., Zhang, Z., Lin, K., Dai, Y., & Yung, K. K. L. (2019). Traditional Chinese medicine-based neurorestorative therapy for Alzheimer's and Parkinson's disease. *Journal of Neurorestoratology*, *7*(4), 207–222. https://doi.org/10.26599/JNR.2019.9040026

# 2 Social Determinants in Human Health

*Nicole W. Y. Fung and Ben Y. F. Fong*

## Introduction

Social determinants of health are defined as "the conditions in which people are born, grow, work, live and age", shaping their daily living and driving positive health outcomes (World Health Organization, 2009). The distribution of power, income and resources, such as access to healthcare and education, are the fundamental causes of health inequities, which are often determined by the social, political, economic, environmental and cultural factors (Braveman & Gottlieb, 2014). Therefore, these non-medical factors pose critical impacts on health-related behaviours and constitute the "social determinants of health", which comprise five domains: economic stability, education access and quality, healthcare access and quality, neighbourhood and built environment, and social and community context (Office of Disease Prevention and Health Promotion, 2020).

Apart from ensuring health equity, the importance of the social determinants of health is further extended to the sustainable development in health. The Sustainable Development Goal 3 (SDG 3) aims to "ensure healthy lives and promote well-being for all at all ages" and is interrelated with health equity (Department of Global Communication of the United Nations, 2023). Research has shown that health equity is critical in enhancing global health outcomes, or universal health coverage advocated strongly by the World Health Organization, with the objective to "leave no one behind" in both the short and long terms and to foster sustainable development of health (Buzeti et al., 2020; Fischer & Carow, 2022).

Despite the efforts in the development of equity and sustainability in health promotion made by organisations and countries in the world, the COVID-19 pandemic has caused significant negative and adverse impacts on the environment, society and other aspects of human lives. According to the data from the World Health Organization (2024a), there were over 775 million reported cases of COVID-19 and more than 7 million deaths worldwide as of 21 April 2024. During the pandemic, it was found that the discrepancies in socioeconomic status, in addition to race and ethnicity, were directly associated with the influences of the pandemic (Abrams & Szefler, 2020; Singu

DOI: 10.4324/9781032701356-2

et al., 2020). Evidence has illustrated that people with low economic status, low income, low education level and other disadvantages were more vulnerable to the attacks by the virus. Other reasons included lower health literacy, poor living environment and reduced accessibility to healthcare services due to the established measures during the COVID-19 pandemic, such as physical distancing and lockdowns.

Moreover, it was observed that older adults and individuals with pre-existing chronic conditions, such as asthma, cardiovascular diseases (CVDs), hypertension, chronic kidney disease (CKD), or obesity, were experiencing higher risk of complications and long COVID-19 once they got infected. A higher infection rate was also found among the minority, and one of the reasons was the challenges for communication. The closure of schools might have further increased the health risks of this particular group during the COVID-19 pandemic as schools normally ensured their food security, but virtual lessons reduced their accessibility to education (Abrams & Szefler, 2020; Singu et al., 2020). These incidents and observations during the pandemic are all pointing to the gross shortcomings of current health systems worldwide, suggesting the importance of addressing the social determinants of health in public health and the community. Therefore, it is critical to evaluate the interrelationships between the social determinants of health and health equity, as well as the sustainable development of health promotion, from the lessons learned from the COVID-19 pandemic and similar outbreaks like SARS.

This review aims to summarise the implementation and development of SDG 3 made by countries and organisations during the COVID-19 pandemic, in light of the five domains of social determinants of health. It also evaluates the current barriers to the implementation and development of sustainable health promotion, particularly the shortage of healthcare professionals and time constraints, and provides relevant recommendations for future directions.

## Five Domains of Social Determinants of Health

The five domains of social determinants of health encompass economic stability, education access and quality, healthcare access and quality, neighbourhood and built environment, and social and community context. These determinants are interrelated and play a major role in the health status of all individuals and communities, in order to support the implementation and development of SDG 3. The impacts of disparities in any of these conditions were noted to be particularly significant during the COVID-19 pandemic (Abrams & Szefler, 2020; Singu et al., 2020).

### *Economic Stability*

The goal of economic stability is to help people attain stable incomes in meeting their social, domestic and health needs (Office of Disease Prevention and Health Promotion, 2020). Employment is the major influencing factor and thus refers to one's income, socioeconomic status and cost of living as well. Poverty, unemployment, underemployment, food insecurity and housing insecurity are directly associated with economic instability and also negative health outcomes (Singu et al., 2020). Furthermore, the type of job, level of income and job benefits, such as health insurance and paid leaves, are mainly determined by one's education level, and sometimes race and ethnicity (Singu et al., 2020). In addition, physical disabilities, injuries or chronic conditions like arthritis are also considered as limiting factors of work abilities (Office of Disease Prevention and Health Promotion, 2020).

Studies have suggested the impacts of education level, socioeconomic status, race and ethnicity, and health conditions on the level of burden of COVID-19 like morbidity and mortality rate (Cross et al., 2022; Green et al., 2021; Singu et al., 2020; Yoshikawa & Kawachi, 2021). During the pandemic, worldwide economic activities were slowed down with the social distancing, quarantine and lockdown measures, and had led to an increase in unemployment and a reduction of income for many people, particularly ethnic minorities, and this further resulted in a higher risk of infection and disease severity (International Labour Organization, & Organization for Economic Cooperation and Development, 2020; Magesh et al., 2021). For example, compared to white individuals, the racial minorities in the United States, Hispanics, African Americans and Asian Americans, were facing a greater probability of unemployment, wage reduction or being forced to take unpaid leave, if they were infected during the COVID-19 pandemic (Magesh et al., 2021; Singu et al., 2020). The wage reduction or job loss exposed them to higher vulnerability to the pandemic due to food insecurity, limited access to healthcare and housing insecurity, not only for the individuals but also for their families and the community (Green et al., 2021).

Moreover, it is suggested that low-income populations might have steady work but insufficient income to maintain healthy living (Office of Disease Prevention and Health Promotion, 2020). This situation is referred to as working poverty or in-work poverty. Employees of essential jobs such as food services, retail, cleaning and sanitation and transport are more vulnerable to infections like COVID-19 (Cabrero, 2010; Chartered Institute of Personal and Development, 2023). During the COVID-19 pandemic, higher infection, hospitalisation and mortality rates were reported in the low-income and low-socioeconomic-status groups (Green et al., 2021; Wachtler et al., 2020). This could be due to the increased chance of exposure to the virus for workers in food services, retail, cleaning and sanitation and transport (Magesh et al., 2021; Singu et al., 2020).

In response to the economic damages of the COVID-19 pandemic, major economies have introduced various fiscal, monetary and financial policies, targeting households, firms, health systems and banks (Rama & Lankes, 2020). For example, direct cash transfers, wage subsidies, consumption coupons for low-income households, unemployment benefits and compensation for sick leave were suggested to be effective supporting measures for workers and households (Elgin et al., 2020). It is important for the governments to address the economic challenges according to the local situations in the form of public support. Besides, more focus should be put on job loss issues (Rama & Lankes, 2020).

Despite the short-term policies in addressing the economic pressures posed by the pandemic, it is in the interest of all governments to introduce long-term measures for the sustainable development of health equity, as well as enhancing health outcomes for the community (Department of Global Communication of the United Nations, 2023). With work types and incomes being highly related to the education level, and significantly associated with access to healthcare services, living environment, time for social activities, as well as the opportunity for education for children, the evidence above has shown that economic stability is the fundamental determinant of health and with effects on the other four domains (Cross et al., 2022; Green et al., 2021; Singu et al., 2020). Therefore, improvements in strategies that support employment, such as job-finding programmes and career counselling, and policies that ensure fair and steady income and job benefits, along with social support on basic daily life needs for all people, are necessary and critical to the development and implementation of health equity and achieving the SDG 3, all from the lessons learned from the pandemic.

### *Education Access and Quality*

The education access and quality domain aims to increase educational opportunities and support the learning process in schools and universities for children and adolescents, in order to help them attain higher education level and language literacy that are key factors for a higher income, as well as enhanced health outcomes later in their lives (Office of Disease Prevention and Health Promotion, 2020; Waddill, 2020). The school environment, household incomes, parental involvement and socioeconomic status are critical determinants of children's academic performances and eventual education level. Studies have suggested that students from low socioeconomic status with little or no parental involvement in their education have limited access to educational resources for facilitating academic achievements and a higher probability of dropping out from high school (Broer et al., 2019; Singu et al., 2020). It is also reported that race and ethnicity is another factor causing educational disparities (Gee et al., 2023).

While schools could be the only access to educational resources for many children from low-income households, school closures arising from the physical distancing measures during the COVID-19 pandemic had posed adverse impacts on their learning and health (Abrams & Szefler, 2020; Gee et al., 2023). Face-to-face teaching was discontinued and replaced by remote learning like virtual lessons during school closures. However, digital devices or the Internet might not be available in the houses of students from low socioeconomic status families, leading them to lose opportunities to access education from schools, not even to mention other online educational resources (Singu et al., 2020). Moreover, without much supplementary support from teachers and classmates, parents became the major navigators of learning. Yet, most of the parents from low-income households had limited education levels compared with those from higher-income families, thus resulting in further disparities in academic achievements during the public health crisis (Gee et al., 2023; Pokhrel & Chhetri, 2021).

In order to facilitate children's access to remote learning, some countries were forced to react to such issues without the necessary infrastructure in place. For example, the government of Peru launched a multimodal strategy combining low-tech and high-tech remote learning platforms to deliver scale learning. Apart from online learning courses, the government cooperated with telecommunication operators to deliver learning programmes in nine native languages through television and radio. Some governments, such as Chile, Columbia, Thailand and Saudi Arabia, have also made agreements with local bandwidth service providers for zero-rated data or subsidised Internet access. Algeria, Bhutan and Iran governments have provided subsidised devices for remote learning to students in need as well (Munoz-Najar et al., 2021). Furthermore, the World Bank provided funding to various countries for adapting and implementing remote learning programmes that covered students of different gender, and race and ethnicity, as well as training for teachers on the delivery of remote learning and hygiene products (Munoz-Najar et al., 2021; World Bank, 2021).

The COVID-19 pandemic has well demonstrated weaknesses of the worldwide education system and reminded authorities of the importance of enhancing equity in education access despite geographic location, socioeconomic status or race and ethnicity, as education access and quality pose significant impacts on students' income, socioeconomic status and health in the future (Gee et al., 2023; Munoz-Najar et al., 2021). It is also shown that schooling is necessary and basic to achieve fair and sustainable development in health promotion. Therefore, provisions of extra educational resources and academic support for students from low socioeconomic status households are critical in facilitating the implementation and achievement of "Health for all" (Broer et al., 2019; Gee et al., 2023).

### *Healthcare Access and Quality*

The healthcare access and quality domain consists of variables that influence access to comprehensive and high-quality healthcare services (Office of Disease Prevention and Health Promotion, 2020). As mentioned previously, poverty is a barrier to accessing high-quality healthcare services in time due to limited financial affordability. Likewise, the increased unemployment rate has led to the loss of health insurance and will raise the financial burden of accessing healthcare services for individuals. In general, poverty implies low income, low education level, low health literacy, limited coverage of health insurance and potential language challenges and disabilities. These factors could link to a greater financial or physical burden in obtaining the necessary healthcare services, as well as the incompetency of receiving essential health information and knowledge, resulting in ineffective communication with healthcare professionals (Tzenios, 2019). Moreover, the quality and availability of healthcare services, particularly in primary care and speciality care, are the other key determinants of healthcare access as well (Singu et al., 2020; Tzenios, 2019).

Research has reported that higher infection, hospitalisation, and death rates among the low-socioeconomic-status group might be due to limited access and literacy to necessary healthcare services, such as pandemic-related information during COVID-19 (Pujolar et al., 2022; Singu et al., 2020; Tzenios, 2019). In addition to insufficient understanding of the diseases due to limited literacy or language challenges, and ineffective communication with healthcare providers, individuals with low socioeconomic status were more vulnerable to the virus as they failed to reach for the necessary healthcare services in time (Tzenios, 2019). The situation was further aggravated for patients with pre-existing chronic conditions and disabilities. To make things worse, the physical distancing and lockdown measures during the pandemic had increased the physical barriers to access healthcare services for such groups of patients and could have negative impacts on their self-efficacy in self-management, leading to further deterioration in health conditions (Pujolar et al., 2022; Singu et al., 2020; Tzenios, 2019).

Access to healthcare has a critical role in controlling the morbidity and mortality rates from the COVID-19 pandemic. Thus, subsidised treatment for high-risk patients including older adults and individuals with disabilities or chronic health conditions was funded by the governments in various countries such as the United States and the United Kingdom (Cole, 2020; National Health Services in England, 2023). On the other hand, the pandemic has fostered the development and implementation of telemedicine in many countries (Omboni et al., 2022). The use of telemedicine could maintain some patient care and reduce the risk of exposure to the virus. However, the lack of comprehensive regulations to monitor the efficacy and quality of telemedicine care and barriers to access for patients with disabilities or other specific health conditions were noted (Núñez et al., 2021; Omboni et al., 2022; Ortega et al., 2020).

The integration of telemedicine and face-to-face consultation could be an effective way to enhance health outcomes in the long term (Omboni et al., 2022). Yet, the COVID-19 pandemic has demonstrated that the current practice of telemedicine is not well prepared and improvements are required to aim for the sustainable development of healthcare.

### *Neighbourhood and Built Environment*

The neighbourhood and built environment domain includes variables that affect the physical living home and surrounding environments and social neighbourhood in the community. Access to healthy food and clean water, quality of housing, access to transportation, crime and violence, air quality and environmental conditions are all influencing factors of neighbourhood and built environment, and they are critical to the physical and mental health of individuals. Ethnical minorities and people with low income have higher chances to live in low-quality neighbourhoods that are characterised by limited options of healthy food, polluted water, higher rates of crime and violence, air pollution, greater smoke exposure and few green spaces available. As a result, such groups face a higher risk of chronic diseases and mental health issues (Office of Disease Prevention and Health Promotion, 2020; Singu et al., 2020).

Studies have evaluated the associations between the population density of the neighbourhood, socioeconomic status and the spread of COVID-19 (Green et al., 2021; Hatef et al., 2020; Zhang et al., 2022). The transmission rate and prevalence of COVID-19 were higher, particularly under the social distancing measures, in disadvantaged neighbourhoods that were crowded with individuals and families of low income, due to the limited living spaces. Moreover, poor hygiene, high exposure to pollution and unhealthy food and limited access to green spaces and exercise facilities during the lockdown period could also lead to higher vulnerability to chronic conditions and the virus against these population groups, causing further negative health outcomes (Hatef et al., 2020; Hong et al., 2021). However, prompt improvements in urban settings during the pandemic were limited, and therefore, community engagement and building resilience were important as a timely response to the pandemic as well as long-term development of more healthy communities (Den Broeder et al., 2022).

As neighbourhoods of low-socioeconomic status are more vulnerable to diseases, particularly to the catastrophic ones like the COVID-19 pandemic, community resilience is critical to empower such groups with the ability of managing and responding to adverse environmental and social conditions. Community engagement is essential to boost up social support, primary care and improvement in urban settings in deprived communities to deliver effective health promotion programmes (Den Broeder et al., 2022; Lau et al., 2021). Therefore, it is revealed by the pandemic that apart from relieving over-crowdedness and enhancing the urban settings of low-income neighbourhoods, the governments should also put extra efforts into social and community development to attain equity in health and sustain sustainable development for effective health promotion for such neighbourhoods (Den Broeder et al., 2022; Hatef et al., 2020).

### *Social and Community Context*

The social and community context domain aims to facilitate mutual support and social cohesion in communities where people live, study, work, relax, grow and age. The sense of belonging to a community or workplace means positive relationships that could link to enhanced well-being for individuals, while racism, discrimination and violence denote negative interactions that could result in negative impacts on health and well-being. Racism and discrimination are also associated with negative impacts on employment, access to education and healthcare, and neighbourhoods (Office of Disease Prevention and Health Promotion, 2020; Singu et al., 2020). Yet, the implementation of social distancing and lockdown measures during the pandemic might hinder the communication between individuals and the communities and result in social isolation and loneliness that were risk factors for psychological issues, particularly for older adults who already had limited mobility and limited social network and connectivity (Kim & Jung, 2021; Marzo et al., 2022; McQuaid et al., 2021).

Research has illustrated that loneliness is linked to depression and anxiety and that low-household incomes were significantly associated with loneliness during the pandemic (McQuaid et al., 2021). While social isolation and loneliness have proven to be associated with negative health impacts, particularly in deprived neighbourhoods prior to the pandemic, limited social activities and face-to-face interactions among individuals from the social distancing and lockdown measures had further exacerbated these effects on mental health, and the well-being of such population groups (Algren et al., 2020; McQuaid et al., 2021). For older adults, interpersonal ties are important to their mental well-being for them to feel connected to the community and receive various information (Birditt et al., 2020). Social distancing and lockdown measures had led to the loss of interpersonal ties, which were also due to the fear of getting infected or death. The consequences were shown by the trend of national mortality (Kim & Jung, 2021). If the national mortality caused by the pandemic was reported in terms of number rather than rate, social distancing and lockdown measures could further amplify the fear among older adults and aggravate their psychological burden caused by social isolation (Kim & Jung, 2021; McQuaid et al., 2021).

Telehealth services have grown promptly and unexpectedly fast worldwide due to COVID-19; in particular, when the time social distancing and lockdown measures were implemented. It has been reported an increased utilisation and application of telehealth in mental health services for patients of different ages, including youth and older adults, during the pandemic could be an effective and safe solution to enhance access to mental support as well as relieving untoward mental stress (Jayawardana & Gannon, 2021; Molfenter et al., 2021). However, many challenges in promoting nationwide telehealth services for all people were identified, such as limited digital literacy, apparently among older adults, and communication barriers for clinical assessments (Shaver, 2022).

The pandemic provided a good showcase on the feasibility of using telehealth services as a solution to enhance the accessibility of healthcare services in ensuring the quality of healthcare services and sustainable development in health promotion, rather than just being a temporary option to deliver healthcare services during the pandemic. In view of the barriers to the promotion of telehealth found during the pandemic, more efforts should be put into the improvement of the telehealth services system and facilitating the implementation. This is a very good example of employing technology to attain advanced health outcomes "for all at all ages".

## Barriers in Sustainable Health Promotion

Apart from the weaknesses of current worldwide healthcare systems regarding the social determinants learned from the COVID-19 pandemic, there are barriers to facilitating sustainable health promotion and development as well. These barriers are related to the lack of Health in All Policies, underdevelopment of primary healthcare, manpower shortage, and time constraints, which also affect transdisciplinary collaboration, research, community engagement and empowerment, and public and health education in schools and workplaces.

### *Lack of Health in All Policies*

To achieve health for all, supportive policies and strategies with respect to the social determinants of health are critical. Whilst as discussed earlier, the COVID-19 pandemic has well-demonstrated the insufficiency and ineffectiveness of relevant public health interventions. Research has illustrated that there are conflicting expectations and demands among different political parties and stakeholders, and their differences in the priority they have given to healthcare (Greer et al., 2022). Therefore, all sectors should hold the similar and concerted understanding of the importance of public health and collaborate for health promotion by adopting the Health in All Policies approach, where health is considered and incorporated into all public policies. The comprehensive and effective implementation of Health in All Policies requires strategic communication between health and other sectors to introduce smart health policies with mutual benefits, thereby providing incentives for the engagement of different sectors (Cain et al., 2022; Greer et al., 2022). All are involved in this matter of public concern, "*Health for All – All for Health*".

### *Underdevelopment of Primary Healthcare*

Primary healthcare is critical in recognising the health-related needs and problems of all individuals in the populations that constitute the society and in achieving improved health outcomes and equity. It also enables more resilient health systems to prepare for, respond to and recover from public health crises like the COVID-19 pandemic, with person-centred and community-based health services (World Health Organization, 2023). However, the damages caused by COVID-19 have provided good evidence of the underdevelopment of global primary healthcare. To facilitate effective primary healthcare, it is important to enhance the accessibility to healthcare services across the population, provide financial support for primary care services and examine the extent of necessity of different healthcare services by the population.

#### *Manpower Shortage*

Healthcare workers are a vital resource in health services and a significant driver in the quality of care and health promotion. However, countries at all levels of socioeconomic development are facing different degrees of shortfalls in healthcare workers (Erestain, 2022). Studies have elaborated that the imbalance of the supply and demand of the healthcare workforce has contributed to the shortage. The increasing international migration of healthcare workers, long time periods in education and training of healthcare workers, the mismatch between the education and employment strategies and the demand of people have led to the shortage of healthcare manpower. On the other hand, the increasing ageing population is positively related to the demand for healthcare workforce and further exacerbates the shortage (Erestain, 2022; World Health Organization, 2024b). As a result, the quality of healthcare services and the overall well-being of healthcare workers are being threatened (Erestain, 2022).

#### *Time Constraint*

An imbalance in the demand and supply of healthcare workers has led to chronic problems in healthcare systems such as long waiting times for consultations and emergency department services, and shortages of hospital beds, which could further result in serious consequences for clinical conditions and increased financial burdens to the healthcare system. Moreover, healthcare providers have to work under pressure to deliver high-quality services in a more efficient way. These problems caused by time constraints hinder the enhancement of health outcomes and the further development of sustainable healthcare services (Bacelar-Silva et al., 2022).

#### *Transdisciplinary Collaboration*

The collaboration between the health sector and other sectors is indispensable to attain health equity and equality through policies. Transdisciplinary collaboration aims to integrate knowledge from research context and perspectives from expertise for setting and producing goals and practices for common goods. This has indicated the necessity of involving team members of different sectors and backgrounds, all stakeholders of the society and the exchange of perspectives (Sell et al., 2022). However, transdisciplinary collaboration emphasises comprehensive communication and understanding among different stakeholders; otherwise, it could lead to inefficiencies in the planning and implementation of health policies (Martin et al., 2023).

#### *Research*

Research is important to provide reliable knowledge regarding the role of social, economic, political, environmental and behavioural forces in determining health outcomes through practices and policies. Knowledge also plays a vital role in transdisciplinary collaboration that facilitates communication among researchers, experts, citizens and policymakers for advancing health policies. Research has yet suggested that such communication is inefficient in achieving the common interests of all parties. Moreover, a lack of proper regulation for facilitating evidence-building, data sharing and knowledge translation could hinder the implementation of research results into practices (Sipido & Nagyova, 2020).

#### *Community Engagement and Empowerment*

The application of five levels of community engagement, consisting of informing, consulting, planning, collaborating and empowering communities, for building community resilience is suggested by the World Health Organization (2020). Community resilience is critical for strengthening individuals and communities to prepare for, respond to and recover from shocks and crises. However, communications among stakeholders are often inefficient due to conflicting interests, thereby hindering the involvement of communities in health decisions and promotion (Aberese-Ako et al., 2024).

#### *Public Education and Health Education in Schools, Universities and Workplaces*

Public education and health education for students and employees are effective and timely approaches to health promotion in the communities. Essential health literacy, knowledge and skills could be transferred to the communities and foster positive behavioural changes in the lifestyle of individuals, thus empowering the next generation and workers, and their families in the communities with improved health and well-being (Auld et al., 2020).

## Concluding Remarks

Evidence of the shortcomings of the current health system is well-established from the COVID-19 pandemic. Therefore, more efforts in the development of policies to address the issues related to the five domains of social determinants of health are critical and urgently needed for enhancing health outcomes for all individuals in the communities and for the sustainable development of healthcare services.

Moreover, to overcome the current barriers to sustainable development of health promotion, efforts from different sectors and all stakeholders are required. Firstly, to enhance health equity through government policy, it is essential for policymakers to take the initiative to plan and implement health equity strategies as well as facilitate the translation of research knowledge into health policies and practices. These could be important to facilitate transdisciplinary collaboration, thereby attaining comprehensive sustainable development in health promotion. Secondly, in order to foster the development of primary healthcare, the governments should address the current challenges for developing comprehensive primary healthcare, facilitate efficient communication with the community, as well as take reference to other countries for empowering the populations with enhanced health resilience through primary healthcare and community engagement. Moreover, effective programmes regarding public education and health education in schools, universities, and workplaces are indispensable to further empower the communities with advanced health literacy and healthy lifestyle changes. More importantly, to reduce the pressure on the limited resources of the healthcare system, including the manpower shortage and time constraints, the relocation and distribution of resources are suggested to facilitate optimal resources management.

The promotion of health for all is critical to enhance health outcomes and sustainable development of not just the healthcare system, but also the well-being of the society. Thus, all stakeholders are responsible for achieving the goal of "health in all", while the authorities should take the initiative.

## References


Aberese-Ako, M., Doegah, P. T., Kpodo, L., Ebelin, W., Kuatewo, M., Baba, A. A., Kpordorlor, A. G., Lissah, S. Y., Kuug, A. K., & Ansah, E. (2024). The role of community engagement toward ensuring healthy lives: A case study of COVID-19 management in two Ghanaian municipalities. *Frontiers in Public Health, 11*, 1213121. https://doi.org/10.3389/fpubh.2023.1213121

Abrams, E. M., & Szefler, S. J. (2020). COVID-19 and the impact of social determinants of health. *The Lancet Respiratory Medicine, 8*(7), 659–661.

Algren, M. H., Ekholm, O., Nielsen, L., Ersbøll, A. K., Bak, C. K., & Andersen, P. T. (2020). Social isolation, loneliness, socioeconomic status, and health-risk behaviour in deprived neighbourhoods in Denmark: A cross-sectional study. *SSM – Population Health, 10*, 100546. https://doi.org/10.1016/j.ssmph.2020.100546

Auld, M. E., Allen, M. P., Hampton, C., Montes, J. H., Sherry, C., Mickalide, A. D., Logan, R. A., Alvarado-Little, W., & Parson, K. (2020). Health literacy and health education in schools: Collaboration for action. *NAM Perspectives, 2020*. https://doi.org/10.31478/202007b

Bacelar-Silva, G. M., Cox III, J. F., & Rodrigues, P. P. (2022). Outcomes of managing healthcare services using the theory of constraints: A systematic review. *Health Systems, 11*(1), 1–16.

Birditt, K. S., Polenick, C. A., Luong, G., Charles, S. T., & Fingerman, K. L. (2020). Daily interpersonal tensions and well-being among older adults: The role of emotion regulation strategies. *Psychology and Aging, 35*(4), 578–590. https://doi.org/10.1037/pag0000416

Braveman, P., & Gottlieb, L. (2014). The social determinants of health: It's time to consider the causes of the causes. *Public Health Reports (Washington, D.C.: 1974), 129*(Suppl 2), 19–31. https://doi.org/10.1177/00333549141291S206

Broer, M., Bai, Y., Fonseca, F., Broer, M., Bai, Y., & Fonseca, F. (2019). A review of the literature on socioeconomic status and educational achievement. In *Socioeconomic inequality and educational outcomes: Evidence from twenty years of TIMSS* (pp. 7–17). Springer.

Buzeti, T., Madureira Lima, J., Yang, L., & Brown, C. (2020). Leaving no one behind: Health equity as a catalyst for the sustainable development goals. *European Journal of Public Health, 30*(Supplement_1), i24–i27.

Cabrero, G. R. (2010). *Spain. In-work poverty and labour market segmentation. A study of national policies.* European Commission. https://ec.europa.eu/social/BlobServlet?docId=9016&langId=en

Cain, R., Greece, J. A., Galea, S., Knight, E. K., Manco, A., Parikh, A., & Jones, D. K. (2022). Improving health across sectors: Best practices for the implementation of health in all policies approaches. *Preventive Medicine Reports, 29*, 101961.

Chartered Institute of Personal and Development. (2023). *Tackling in-work poverty: Guidance for employers.* Chartered Institute of Personal and Development. www.cipd.org/en/knowledge/guides/in-work-poverty/#:~:text=What%20is%20in%2Dwork%20poverty%3F,-In%2Dwork%20poverty&text=In%2Dwork%20poverty%20occurs%20when,households%20below%20average%20income%20statistics

Cole, B. (2020). The impact of the COVID-19 pandemic on access to health care. *Health Policy Brief, 17*, 1–31.

Cross, K., Evans, J., MacLeavy, J., & Manley, D. (2022). Analysing the socio-economic impacts of COVID-19: A new regional geography or pandemic enhanced inequalities? *Regional Studies, Regional Science, 9*(1), 461–485. https://doi.org/10.1080/21681376.2022.2084447

Den Broeder, L., South, J., Rothoff, A., Bagnall, A. M., Azarhoosh, F., Van Der Linden, G., Bharadwa, M., & Wagemakers, A. (2022). Community engagement in deprived neighbourhoods during the COVID-19 crisis: Perspectives for more resilient and healthier communities. *Health Promotion International, 37*(2), daab098.

Department of Global Communication of the United Nations. (2023). *What is goal 3 – Good health and well-being.* Department of Global Communication of the United Nations. www.un.org/sustainabledevelopment/wp-content/uploads/2023/09/Goal-3_Fast-Facts.pdf

Elgin, C., Basbug, G., & Yalaman, A. (2020). Economic policy responses to a pandemic: Developing the COVID-19 economic stimulus index. *Covid Economics, 1*(3), 40–53.

Erestain, L. (2022). *The impact of manpower shortage in the healthcare industry.* LAB Universities of Applied Sciences. www.theseus.fi/bitstream/handle/10024/783260/Erestain_Lovilla.pdf?sequence=2&isAllowed=y

Fischer, F., & Carow, F. (2022). Impact of public health and sustainability of global health action for achieving SDG 3. In *Transitioning to good health and well-being* (pp. 111–132). Mdpi AG.

Gee, K. A., Asmundson, V., & Vang, T. (2023). Educational impacts of the COVID-19 pandemic in the United States: Inequities by race, ethnicity, and socioeconomic status. *Current Opinion in Psychology, 52*, 101643.

Green, H., Fernandez, R., & MacPhail, C. (2021). The social determinants of health and health outcomes among adults during the COVID-19 pandemic: A systematic review. *Public Health Nursing (Boston, Mass.), 38*(6), 942–952. https://doi.org/10.1111/phn.12959

Greer, S. L., Falkenbach, M., Siciliani, L., McKee, M., Wismar, M., & Figueras, J. (2022). From health in all policies to health for all policies. *The Lancet Public Health, 7*(8), e718–e720.

Hatef, E., Chang, H. Y., Kitchen, C., Weiner, J. P., & Kharrazi, H. (2020). Assessing the impact of neighborhood socioeconomic characteristics on COVID-19 prevalence across seven states in the United States. *Frontiers in Public Health, 8*, 571808.

Hong, B., Bonczak, B. J., Gupta, A., Thorpe, L. E., & Kontokosta, C. E. (2021). Exposure density and neighborhood disparities in COVID-19 infection risk. *Proceedings of the National Academy of Sciences, 118*(13), e2021258118.

International Labour Organization, & Organization for Economic Cooperation and Development. (2020). *The impact of the COVID-19 pandemic on jobs and incomes in G20 economies.* ILO-OECD Paper Prepared at the Request of G20 Leaders, Saudi Arabia's G20 Presidency (pp. 1–46). G20 Saudi Arabia.

Jayawardana, D., & Gannon, B. (2021). Use of telehealth mental health services during the COVID-19 pandemic. *Australian Health Review*, *45*(4), 442–446.

Kim, H. H. S., & Jung, J. H. (2021). Social isolation and psychological distress during the COVID-19 pandemic: A cross-national analysis. *The Gerontologist*, *61*(1), 103–113.

Lau, S. M., Chan, Y. C., Fung, K. K., Hung, S. L., & Feng, J. (2021). Hong Kong under COVID-19: Roles of community development service. *International Social Work*, *64*(2), 270–274. https://doi.org/10.1177/0020872820967734

Magesh, S., John, D., Li, W. T., Li, Y., Mattingly-App, A., Jain, S., Chang, E. Y., & Ongkeko, W. M. (2021). Disparities in COVID-19 outcomes by race, ethnicity, and socioeconomic status: A systematic review and meta-analysis. *JAMA Network Open*, *4*(11), e2134147–e2134147.

Martin, A. K., Green, T. L., McCarthy, A. L., Sowa, P. M., & Laakso, E. L. (2023). Allied health transdisciplinary models of care in hospital settings: A scoping review. *Journal of Interprofessional Care*, *37*(1), 118–130.

Marzo, R. R., Khanal, P., Ahmad, A., Rathore, F. A., Chauhan, S., Singh, A., Shrstha, S., AlRifai, A., Lotfizadeh, M., Younus, D. A., Billah, M. A., Rahman, F., Sivaladchanam, Y., Mohan, D., & Su, T. T. (2022). Quality of life of the elderly during the COVID-19 pandemic in Asian countries: A cross-sectional study across six countries. *Life*, *12*(3), 365.

McQuaid, R. J., Cox, S. M., Ogunlana, A., & Jaworska, N. (2021). The burden of loneliness: Implications of the social determinants of health during COVID-19. *Psychiatry Research*, *296*, 113648.

Molfenter, T., Heitkamp, T., Murphy, A. A., Tapscott, S., Behlman, S., & Cody, O. J. (2021). Use of telehealth in mental health (MH) services during and after COVID-19. *Community Mental Health Journal*, *57*(7), 1244–1251.

Munoz-Najar, A., Gilberto, A., Hasan, A., Cobo, C., Azevedo, J. P., & Akmal, M. (2021). *Remote learning during COVID-19: Lessons from today, principles for tomorrow*. World Bank Group. https://www.worldbank.org/en/topic/edutech/brief/how-countries-are-using-edtech-to-support-remote-learning-during-the-covid-19-pandemic

National Health Services in England. (2023). Access to COVID treatments. *National Health Services inEngland*. www.england.nhs.uk/coronavirus/documents/access-to-covid-treatments/

Núñez, A., Sreeganga, S. D., & Ramaprasad, A. (2021). Access to healthcare during COVID-19. *International Journal of Environmental Research and Public Health*, *18*(6), 2980

Office of Disease Prevention and Health Promotion. (2020). *Social determinants of health-what are the social determinants of health?* Office of Disease Prevention and Health Promotion. https://health.gov/healthypeople/priority-areas/social-determinants-health

Omboni, S., Padwal, R. S., Alessa, T., Benczúr, B., Green, B. B., Hubbard, I., Kario, K., Khan, N. A., Konradi, A., Logan, A. G., Lu, Y., Mars, M., McManus, R. J., Melville, S., Neumann, C. L., Parati, G., Renna, N. F., Ryvlin, P., Saner, H., . . . & Wang, J. (2022). The worldwide impact of telemedicine during COVID-19: Current evidence and recommendations for the future. *Connected Health*, *1*, 7–35. https://doi.org/10.20517/ch.2021.03

Ortega, G., Rodriguez, J. A., Maurer, L. R., Witt, E. E., Perez, N., Reich, A., & Bates, D. W. (2020). Telemedicine, COVID-19, and disparities: Policy implications. *Health Policy and Technology*, *9*(3), 368–371.

Pokhrel, S., & Chhetri, R. (2021). A literature review on impact of COVID-19 pandemic on teaching and learning. *Higher Education for the Future*, *8*(1), 133–141. https://doi.org/10.1177/2347631120983481

Pujolar, G., Oliver-Anglès, A., Vargas, I., & Vázquez, M. L. (2022). Changes in access to health services during the COVID-19 pandemic: A scoping review. *International Journal of Environmental Research and Public Health*, *19*(3), 1749.

Rama, M. G., & Lankes, H. P. (2020). *The economic policy response to the Covid-19 crisis: Note for discussion*. World Bank Group. https://documents1.worldbank.org/curated/en/694541596107557521/pdf/The-Economic-Policy-Response-to-the-Covid-19-Crisis-Note-for-Discussion.pdf

Sell, K., Hommes, F., Fischer, F., & Arnold, L. (2022). Multi-, Inter-, and transdisciplinarity within the public health workforce: A scoping review to assess definitions and applications of concepts. *International Journal of Environmental Research and Public Health, 19*(17), 10902. https://doi.org/10.3390/ijerph191710902

Shaver, J. (2022). The state of telehealth before and after the COVID-19 pandemic. *Primary Care, 49*(4), 517–530. https://doi.org/10.1016/j.pop.2022.04.002

Singu, S., Acharya, A., Challagundla, K., & Byrareddy, S. N. (2020). Impact of social determinants of health on the emerging COVID-19 pandemic in the United States. *Frontiers in Public Health, 8*, 564623.

Sipido, K. R., & Nagyova, I. (2020). Health research and knowledge translation for achieving the sustainable development goals: Tackling the hurdles. *European Journal of Public Health, 30*(Supplement_1), i36–i40.

Tzenios, N. (2019). The determinants of access to healthcare: A review of individual, structural, and systemic factors. *Journal of Humanities and Applied Science Research, 2*(1), 1–14.

Wachtler, B., Michalski, N., Nowossadeck, E., Diercke, M., Wahrendorf, M., Santos-Hövener, C., Lampert, T., & Hoebel, J. (2020). Socioeconomic inequalities and COVID-19 – A review of the current international literature. *Journal of Health Monitoring, 5*(Suppl 7), 3–17. https://doi.org/10.25646/7059

Waddill, K. (2020). *Top 5 social determinants of health domains for payers to address*. Health Payer Intelligence. https://healthpayerintelligence.com/news/top-5-social-determinants-of-health-domains-for-payers-to-address

World Bank. (2021). *Protecting children from learning loss: Sierra Leone's experience with distance learning and keeping all students safe*. World Bank. www.worldbank.org/en/results/2021/03/17/protecting-children-from-learning-loss-sierra-leone-sexperience-with-distance-learning-and-keeping-all-students-safe

World Health Organization. (2009). *Commission on social determinants of Health*. World Health Organization. https://apps.who.int/gb/ebwha/pdf_files/A62/A62_9-en.pdf

World Health Organization. (2020). *COVID-19 global risk communication and community engagement strategy – interim guidance*. World Health Organization. www.who.int/publications/i/item/covid-19-global-risk-communication-and-community-engagement-strategy

World Health Organization. (2023). *Primary health care*. World Health Organization. www.who.int/news-room/fact-sheets/detail/primary-health-care

World Health Organization. (2024a). *WHO COVID-19 dashboard*. World Health Organization. https://data.who.int/dashboards/covid19/deaths?n=o

World Health Organization. (2024b). *Health workforce*. World Health Organization. www.who.int/health-topics/health-workforce#tab=tab_1

Yoshikawa, Y., & Kawachi, I. (2021). Association of socioeconomic characteristics with disparities in COVID-19 outcomes in Japan. *JAMA Network Open, 4*(7), e2117060–e2117060.

Zhang, A., Shi, W., Tong, C., Zhu, X., Liu, Y., Liu, Z., Yao, Z., & Shi, Z. (2022). The fine-scale associations between socioeconomic status, density, functionality, and spread of COVID-19 within a high-density city. *BMC Infectious Diseases, 22*(1), 274.

# 3 Health Promotion Practices and the Sustainable Global Economy

*Tiffany Cheng Han Leung and Kelly Jialin Xie*

## Health Promotion Practices and SDGs

### *Response and Implementation of the SDGs by the Healthcare Sector*

The holistic and extensive initiation of 17 sustainable development goals (SDGs) and 169 targets in 2015 underpin the conceptual framework for various industries to align their practices and contribution to sustainability, simultaneously, human wellness, economic prosperity, and environmental protection. The United Nations (2015) states that the healthcare sector is at the frontier for health promotion and universal health coverage, which enables people to increase control over and improve their health status. The healthcare sector strives to advance the progressions of health promotion and coverage globally (SDG 3), where the healthcare sector includes not only healthcare products and services companies that manufacture or distribute healthcare-related equipment, supplies and services but also companies associated with medical research, development, production, and marketing of pharmaceutical and biotechnology products (S&P, 2023).

Collectively, the healthcare sector attempts to contribute to the following aspects of SDGs (Table 3.1): (1) access to medicines and healthcare: the efforts to remove barriers and address inequities associated with access to healthcare products and services in developing countries and underserved markets; (2) affordability and pricing: the cost containment against unethical price raising, contractual advantages, and reverse payments to protect patients' rights; (3) product safety and quality: ensure the quality of medical products and services to safeguard the safety of patients; (4) human capital development: the commitment to providing inclusive and equitable quality education and learning opportunities for all regardless of gender, age, and religion; (5) labour management: the dedication to promoting full and productive rights and benefits for employees (MSCI, 2023; The United Nations, 2023a).

### *Health Promotion Practices and SDGs Enablers*

The seamless interactions and interdependences among the 17 SDGs encourage the healthcare sector to identify and examine the attribution to health promotion practices (Costanza et al., 2016; Leung et al., 2023; Rickels et al.,

DOI: 10.4324/9781032701356-3

*Table 3.1* Response of the Healthcare Sector to Relevant SDGs

| *Aspect* | *Response* | *Relevant SDGs* |
|---|---|---|
| Access to Medicines and Healthcare | • To increase underrepresented patients in clinical trials to expand the scope of health services<br>• To donate medicines and funds to charities<br>• To contribute to the World Intellectual Property Organization's Patent Information Initiative for Medicines (Pat-INFORMED) database for direct communication between seekers and companies selling medicines they need<br>• To conduct research and development to address unmet medical needs and neglected diseases | • Goal 3: Ensure healthy lives and promote well-being for all at all ages |
| Affordability and Pricing | • To provide co-pay assistance with commercial insurance<br>• To make donations to independent charitable donation<br>• To develop assistance programmes to provide free medicines to poverty-qualified patients | • Goal 3: Ensure healthy lives and promote well-being for all at all ages |
| Product Safety and Quality | • To uphold applicable quality standards<br>• To prevent drug counterfeiting and medical misconduct | • Goal 3: Ensure healthy lives and promote well-being for all at all ages |
| Human Capital Development | • To cultivate a diverse and inclusive workforce<br>• To ensure gender parity at the leadership level<br>• To instil an inclusive attitude at all levels<br>• To find and engage top talents<br>• To create equal opportunities, develop mentorship and sponsorship for talents to thrive, and pursue personal goals<br>• To leverage strategic partnerships with organisations and educational institutions<br>• To employ underrepresented populations or people with disabilities | • Goal 4: Ensure inclusive and equitable quality education and promote lifelong learning opportunities for all<br>• Goal 5: Achieve gender equality and empower all women and girls<br>• Goal 8: Promote inclusive and sustainable economic growth, full and productive employment, and decent work for all |

(*Continued*)

*Table 3.1* (Continued)

| *Aspect* | *Response* | *Relevant SDGs* |
|---|---|---|
| Labour Management | • To develop an Employee Assistance Programme (EAP) with sufficient resources that support the physical, mental, emotional, financial, workplace, and personal needs<br>• To ensure pay is equitably fair for all employees regardless of gender and race and ethnicity<br>• To respect individual rights, prohibit child labour, forced labour, involuntary labour, human trafficking, and unfair wages and benefits | • Goal 8. Promote inclusive and sustainable economic growth, full and productive employment, and decent work for all<br>• Goal 10. Reduce inequality within and among countries |

*Source:* Biogen (2023), IQVIA (2023), and The United Nations (2023a)

2016). One lesson learned from the chaos, also considered as public health crisis, is that extreme weather, armed conflicts, and the global pandemic contribute to the cost fluctuation as well as pricing fluctuation of health promotion practices. Therefore, this affects the affordability and accessibility of the population to health promotion practices and hence personal wellness. It also results in possible widespread consequences and system collapse at both the national and global scales, which undercut the progress of SDGs. The COVID-19 pandemic has shown the healthcare sector, the community and policymakers the downsides of failing health promotion practices, such as decreasing access and affordability of medicines and healthcare services, resulting in increasing morbidity and death rates, but it has also brought the opportunity for change and advancement for risk assessment for the healthcare system. Accordingly, the healthcare sector interacts and cooperates with other sectors to overcome multiple challenges associated with SDGs, particularly the climate change adaptation and mitigation response (Schmidt et al., 2015), economic development (Ibisch et al., 2016), environmental sustainability, and social inclusion for human wellness (Sachs et al., 2017). Hence, it harnesses the healthcare sector to achieve SDGs through renewable energy infrastructure construction (SDG 7), innovation (SDG 9), sustainable consumption and promotion (SDG12), and reformation and cooperation (SDG 17) (Figure 3.1).

## Energy Infrastructure Gatekeeping and Gaps: Energy Structure Brings New Challenges for Health Promotion Services Delivery

Health programmes reflect the unique contexts and resources of a particular area. Today, on the other hand, health programmes are impactfully shaped by a set of influential megatrends, demanding reformation, and resource

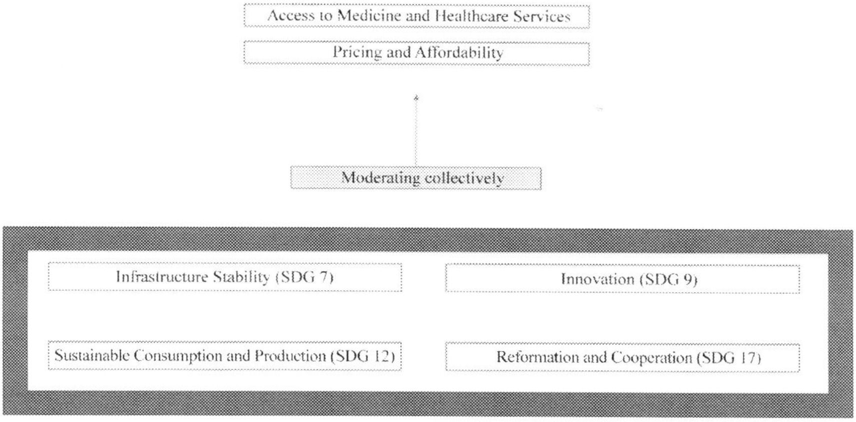


*Figure 3.1* Interaction among SDGs

*Source:* Ibisch et al. (2016); Sachs et al. (2017); Schmidt et al. (2015); The United Nations (2023a)

allocation to deliver health products and services and to meet the expectations and needs of the community. The current situation has shown the healthcare sector and policymakers could take the opportunity to reshape the energy infrastructure, as the collective impacts of climate change, increasing energy prices, and energy supply instability increase the complexity of conducting healthcare-related activities and ultimately threaten people's welfare. This section identifies the drivers behind green infrastructure and how it helps the healthcare sector attain SDG 7 and mitigate climate change. Table 3.2 captures the interrelationship and impacts of climate change and green energy infrastructure as it demonstrates the lagging positions in healthcare regarding energy consumption and infrastructure construction, exposing the fragility of the healthcare system (Amankwah-Amoah, 2020; Asongu et al., 2020; Diop et al., 2020).

### *The Need for Green Infrastructure*

Some studies alarm societies that climate change is the greatest threat to the health of the twenty-first century as it stresses significant strain on health programmes by increasing demand for services and products and creating challenges in energy supply (Costello et al., 2009; Lancet, 2009). Climate change disrupts the delicate stability of health programmes and limits the accessibility of the general public to medical services. Some studies state that the capacity, stability and sustainability of energy supply are inevitably critical for the healthcare sector to deliver products and services, hence promoting health and improving life expectancy (Akinyele, 2017). Extreme circumstances (e.g., rising temperature, floods and earthquakes) reinforce energy poverty, delay patients from receiving medical

*Table 3.2* Potential Impacts of Energy on the Healthcare Sector

| *Main Energy Sources* | *Oil* | *Natural Gas* | *Electricity* |
|---|---|---|---|
| Impacts | Climate Change | Overwhelming Medical Demands | |
| Drivers for Energy Transition | GHG Emission Reduction | Energy Price Increase | Medical Service Stability |
| Affected Parties | Healthcare Facilities | Healthcare Product and Service Providers | Patients and Healthcare Receivers |
| Consequences | ↑ Equipment Failures | ↓ Performance | ↓ Productivity |
| Mitigation Measures | Green Energy Integration | Green Energy Investment | Consumption Optimisation |

*Source*: Authors

products and services, and amplify disparities and socio-economic inequalities, preventing the healthcare sector from advancing SDGs (Dawkins et al., 2021). Consequently, increasing the resilience and stability of energy infrastructure is crucial to ensure the competency of health programmes as the first responders to climate change, overwhelming health challenges and demands and safeguarding health accessibility for the general public. Three major factors are driving the energy infrastructure reconstruction, namely greenhouse gas (GHG) emission reduction, energy price increase, and quality control.

### *GHG Emission Reduction*

The global energy source mix is still substantially dominated by fossil fuels, for example, petroleum and natural gas (Borzuei et al., 2022; Siciliano et al., 2021). Such an energy source is carbon-intensive, accelerating GHG emissions.

Interestingly, Vohra et al. (2021) show that fossil fuel emissions are a leading cause of harming personal health and wellness, pressuring the healthcare sector to reform their energy construction. According to the World Bank (2023b), the healthcare sector is currently estimated to contribute to at least 5% of global GHG emissions. Nevertheless, GHG emissions are a health risk multiplier that contributes to heat-related illnesses and global public health crises in the long run, which forces the healthcare sector in response to reduce GHG emissions. As such, green energy source integration is a sensible and rational move for the healthcare sector against the adverse impacts of GHG emissions. Actions need to be implemented in the healthcare sector to adopt and invest in renewable energy and increase energy efficiency to decrease its environmental footprints proactively from raw material sourcing to end of life (Akinyele et al., 2016; Slater & Bartlett, 2023).

### *Energy Price Increase*

The healthcare sector spends thousands of dollars per bed on energy payments (Vallathan et al., 2022). The price of energy, particularly oil, increases gradually, creating uncertainty in operational costs for the healthcare sector and ultimately increasing the costs of product and service delivery. In developing countries, most clinics that depend on diesel or gasoline-powered generators can only operate temporarily due to the increasing operational expenses. Notably, the healthcare sector uses oil, natural gas, and electricity in many aspects, namely system computation, medical services, medicine production, and other processes for good-quality services. Therefore, the healthcare sector should take measures to reduce unnecessary energy consumption and optimise energy usage efficiency for cost control. Ultimately, the healthcare sector should shift its focus to green energy integration and investment as some studies have shown green energy can achieve cost and emission reduction by 28% and 54%, respectively (Dufo-Lópeza et al., 2016).

### *Medical Service Stability*

The healthcare sector requires a specific, stable, and resilient energy supply to operate the equipment and facilities and enable all energy-consuming-related activities, namely reliable electricity for water supply, temperature control, lighting, and ventilation (Babatunde et al., 2019). Currently, inadequate and unstable energy supply is a frequent and predominant issue in medical services delivery even in developed cities and regions. Despite the availability of pioneering medical equipment and technology, the accessibility and universality of reliable, modern, and green energy are critical for their operation and contribution to reality (Adair-Rohani et al., 2013). The current energy infrastructure limits the ability of the healthcare sector to confront the challenges and changes, consequently hindering the stability of medical services, resulting in equipment failures, and decreasing performance and productivity. Healthcare companies and organisations should request their suppliers for a transition to green energy infrastructure to ensure the stability of medical services and the wellness of recipients.

***Energy Transition Trends: Future Proofing***

As Table 3.3 demonstrates, current energy infrastructure fails to overcome the issues of equipment failures, decreasing performance and productivity of the healthcare sector and future-proof against the increasing complexity of the healthcare services delivery. The healthcare sector proactively encourages companies to restructure their energy infrastructure against climate change, harness their ability to respond to future health emergencies and enhance crisis preparedness. Notably, some healthcare companies and facilities have responded ambitiously, significantly improving their carbon footprint and contribution to SDG 7, substantially increasing shares of green energy in the energy mix globally (Table 3.3).

*User-end: Green Energy Integration*

Energy supply is a diverse mix of energy sources from various system architectures. Healthcare companies are increasingly aware of and participate in green energy integration to address climate change. As such, companies reconstruct their energy infrastructure and technologies to facilitate the process of energy infrastructure reconstruction to decrease the consumption ratio of fossil fuels. Such measures include onsite generation via solar panels and direct purchase of green power (Perera et al., 2019; Vohra et al., 2021).

*Supplier-end: Green Energy Investment*

Likewise, investments in renewable energy are observed in the healthcare sector, where companies have invested in building onsite green energy facilities, such as solar or polar energy storage devices. They can even co-invest with energy supply companies to expand the market and the availability of green

*Table 3.3* Future Trends and Associated SDG 7

| *Aspect* | *Associated SDG 7* |
|---|---|
| Green Energy Integration | • 7.2 By 2030, increase substantially the share of renewable energy in the global energy mix |
| Green Energy Investment | • 7.1 By 2030, ensure universal access to affordable, reliable, and modern energy services<br>• 7.2 By 2030, increase substantially the share of renewable energy in the global energy mix<br>• 7.a By 2030, enhance international cooperation to facilitate access to clean energy research and technology, including renewable energy, energy efficiency, and advanced and cleaner fossil-fuel technology, and promote investment in energy infrastructure and clean energy technology |

*Source*: The United Nations (2023a)

energy, addressing the aggravating state of climate complications. Accordingly, it is recommended to invest in creating more green energy generators, namely wind, solar and hydro, into the global energy mix so that more sufficient and green energy output can be produced and distributed, decreasing environmental and social impact from climate change as well as hedging against the upcoming energy crisis.

## Innovations for Accelerating Healthcare Development

Science and innovation are critical elements of the healthcare sector when responding to public health crises. There were several breakthroughs during COVID-19, reducing the lagging effects in research and reality along with the constant dynamic of changes. Still, much more is needed to remove barriers in research and drive pioneering achievements globally. COVID-19 has highlighted the vulnerability and inaccessibility of the healthcare sector, particularly healthcare facilities and services. The World Bank (2023a) suggests digital innovation can facilitate the adaptation of the healthcare sector to growing and shifting challenges. The successful cases of countries that digitalised health services and implemented digital innovation, for instance, online consultation, had shown the immersive values of digital innovation in healthcare to deliver high-quality, timely and seamless services to the general public against the issue of limited fiscal space and restricted social distancing. Previous studies have stated that innovation, including digital and scientific, has disrupted and revolutionised the healthcare sector threefold: (1) productivity: optimising workflow and improving health financing; (2) accessibility: expanding medical access to underserved communities and focusing on unattained medical needs; and (3) performance: personalising treatment and reducing medical error (Budd et al., 2020; WHO, 2020; Xiong et al., 2023).

### *Innovation to Improve Accessibility and Performance*

Health systems face growing challenges and demands. Nevertheless, the connectivity and accessibility of medical resources demand reform. Baudier et al. (2023) state that digital health innovation has been recognised as a solution to the issues mentioned earlier before COVID-19. Until COVID-19, digital innovations were essentially and rapidly implemented to increase digital connectivity to reach patients (Figure 3.2). The healthcare sector saw substantial progression in healthcare service delivery, where the traditional face-to-face doctor appointment became problematic. Heinrichs et al. (2022) find that digital innovation and adoption can facilitate health system resilience and future health crisis preparedness, encouraging the healthcare sector to use digital innovation for healthcare services provision, healthcare promotion, and administration, accelerating the growth of digital innovation implementation in the medical use (Budd et al., 2020; Golinelli et al., 2020).

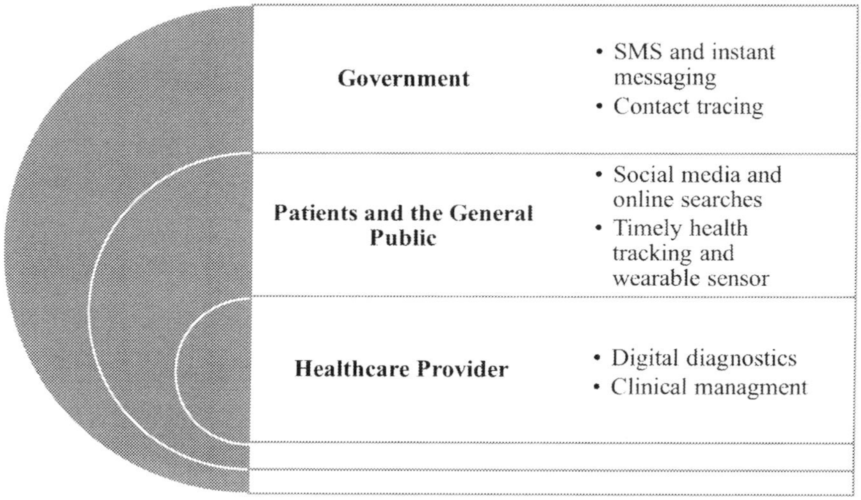


*Figure 3.2* Healthcare Digitalisation
*Source*: Budd et al. (2020); Heinrichs et al. (2022)

Previously, the healthcare sector focused on digitalising workflows, processes, and medical data, and eventually creating information systems to manage. Later, it shifted to application mobilisation to make seamless access against the territory and inequality. However, health promotion practitioners and patients still prefer using such digital innovation for administrative process optimisation, such as client identification and registration, appointment scheduling and medical data access, but not yet unlocking the true potential of digital innovation in diagnostic or clinical care due to a lack of trust and familiarity. The suddenness and overwhelmingness of the COVID-19 pandemic have driven the healthcare sector to four major areas: (1) to upgrade or expand digital infrastructure to increase connectivity to facilities, health professionals and patients; (2) to seek and identify appropriate technological and digital solutions to ensure continuity and accessibility of health promotion services; (3) to provide instructions for digital solution and build digital awareness and skills to increase familiarity; and (4) to improve the monitoring process to ensure trustworthiness (WHO, 2020).

Currently, the healthcare sector is experiencing the digital innovation awakening period and redirecting the focus to digital health, where the knowledge, technology and practices of digital innovation, such as smart devices, the Internet of Things (IoT), and artificial intelligence (AI), are applied to improve health from the clinical and diagnostic side (WHO, 2020; Xiong et al., 2023). Notably, the healthcare sector and associated parties have harnessed the power of digital innovation to enable the development and viability of the healthcare sector (Osei-Frimpong et al., 2015). Table 3.4 shows digital health intervention capturing the current undergoing digital exploration in

*Table 3.4* Digital Health Intervention

| *Aspect* | *Digital Intervention* |
|---|---|
| Diagnostics | • Telemedicine: remote medical consultants, care management, and coordination |
| Surgical | • Robotic, remote site, targeting devices |
| Treatment and devices | • Wearable and implantable devices:tracking, monitoring, and triggering<br>• 3D printing, genetic-based tailoring<br>• New digital therapeutics; virtual and augmented reality for pain management |
| Health Information | • Digitalised records; diagnostics dashboard |
| Generative AI | • Medical chatbots; medical record summarisation<br>• AI/ML knowledge generation |
| Medical Training | • Virtual reality and augmented reality |

*Source*: Osei-Frimpong et al. (2015); WHO (2020); Xiong et al. (2023)

*Table 3.5* Stages of Digital Innovation in the Healthcare Sector

| *Stages* | *Patients and the General Public* | *Healthcare Services Provider* | *Healthcare Product Manufacturer* | *Governments* |
|---|---|---|---|---|
| Digitalisation | Digitalise Processes and Workflows<br>"Improve effectiveness and efficiency of the healthcare sector"<br>↓ | | | |
| Intervention | Integrating with Clinical and Diagnostic Care<br>"Removing barriers and increasing accessibility" | | | |

*Source*: Heinrichs et al. (2022)

reality, where digital innovation is integrated to upgrade digital infrastructure for better and more accessible health promotion services. Table 3.5 summarises the two stages of digital development in the healthcare sector, namely digitalisation and intervention. Digital interventions will enable the healthcare sector to increase the accessibility and quality of healthcare services.

### *Unlocking Pioneering Results for Better Health*

Technology and innovation advancement are at the forefront of research and development in the healthcare sector, particularly in the pharmaceutical and biotechnology industries. As digital innovation advances, the healthcare sector progressively leverages technology-enabled innovation and capacities to advance medical research and shorten the time between research and marketing, where they will simplify the discover-to-distribution timeline and reduce the complexity within the medical development process and ultimately address inherent research challenges and optimise the outcomes for patients and the general public.

*Table 3.6* Innovation Application and Associated SDG 9

| *Aspect* | *Associated SDG 9* |
|---|---|
| Digitalisation | • 9.4 By 2030, upgrade infrastructure and retrofit industries to make them sustainable, with increased resource-use efficiency and greater adoption of clean and environmentally sound technologies and industrial processes, with all countries taking action in accordance with their respective capabilities |
| Innovation Implementation | • 9.5 Enhance scientific research, upgrade the technological capabilities of industrial sectors in all countries, in particular developing countries, including, by 2030, encouraging innovation and substantially increasing the number of research and development workers per 1 million people and public and private research and development spending |

*Source*: The United Nations (2023a)

Wong et al. (2019) state that using biomarkers or other digital innovations will help yield a higher medical research success rate and lower research costs, creating immediate value for the sector and the general public. Notably, there are increasing collaborative and integrated research and solutions, removing complexity and inefficiencies from the process of discovery-to-distribution. Likewise, AI-powered and ML-powered technologies help discover, conceptualise, research, and develop medical solutions. These innovations contribute to discovering new medical needs, repurposing existing medicines, anticipating interactives with other medicines, screening trials, undertaking quality assurance, and monitoring adverse events (Paul et al., 2020). Beyond pharmaceutical and biotechnology development, digital innovations, such as digital diagnostic tools and imaging, have the potential to optimise limited resources and improve accessibility, availability and affordability of quality diagnostics and healthcare services in promoting health and wellness. AI also undertakes the responsibility of cultivating understanding and awareness of (1) diseases from a molecular network and genetic perspectives; (2) medicines, treatment and their impact; and (3) disease severity and personalised supplementation regimens (Doherty et al., 2021).

Digital innovation and technology will help improve health and fundamentally change healthcare with an orientation of SDG 9 (Table 3.6). Greater connectivity, advanced technology utilisation, and digital intervention will unlock the potential of health promotion products and services and create pioneering results for better health, which will help prevent diseases, personalise treatment, and increase affordability.

## Sustainable Consumption and Health Promotion in Practice

The term sustainable consumption is becoming progressively popularised and elaborated as society and consumers have realised resources of the earth are finite and its capacity to re-absorb the by-products of production and waste generation processes is also limited (Gasper et al., 2019). Therefore, the world is constantly advocating sustainable consumption and production to safeguard ecosystems for future generations against ever-increasing production and consumption patterns (The United Nations, 2002). The healthcare sector improves human health and welfare but builds upon a large environmental and material footprint, which needs to be substantially reduced to achieve SDG 12. Schmidheiny (1992) encouraged the healthcare sectors to see sustainability as a business opportunity, not as an existential threat or trade-off. Correspondingly, the healthcare sector aims to reconsolidate environmental protection and economic growth by re-engineering the processes of consumption and production to increase their profitability and reduce their adverse impacts. Unfortunately, most health-related products are single-use products, which cannot be recycled, reused, or even repurposed in the spirit of the circular economy due to hygiene and medical concerns. Therefore, the healthcare sector attempts to uphold the concepts of "Cradle to Grave", reducing the adverse impacts of medical production throughout the stages of raw material extraction, manufacturing and processing, transportation and logistics, usage and retail, and waste disposal. Currently, medical waste management and green chemistry are drawing rising attention in the healthcare sector as they provide the tools for sustainable production and consumption, ultimately contributing to SDG 12.

### *Medical Waste Management*

All individuals who are exposed to medical waste are potentially at risk of infections and diseases. On the other hand, improper or illegal medical waste disposal can lead to pollution, threatening human survivorship and biodiversity (Romero & Carnero, 2019; Wei et al., 2021). Collectively, SDG 3 and SDG 12 advocate that the healthcare sector manage medical waste carefully to protect the general public and environment from hazardous chemicals, air, water and soil pollution and contamination. Medical waste management within healthcare facilities is increasingly examined by stakeholders as it has the potential for environmental contamination, toxic or carcinogenic emissions, affecting society and the environment negatively. Notably, healthcare companies and healthcare professionals are increasingly recognising the urgency and essence of proper medical waste management.

### *General Definition and Classification*

To refine the medical waste management process, the healthcare sector should identify all possible sources and types of medical waste. Medical waste includes waste generated within healthcare facilities, research centres, laboratories, mortuary and autopsy centres, animal research, and blood banks. Medical waste has the likelihood of causing infection and health hazards, demanding careful treatment and strict management to prevent infection to handlers and harm to the community and environment. Medical waste management varies according to the chemical, biological, and medical nature that dictates the modes of disposal. The WHO (2014) indicates that the identification and classification of medical waste is the first step for safe collection, disposal, and management. Classification of medical waste is summarised in Table 3.7.

Interestingly, there is a type of medical waste that exists due to poor inventory management. As such, medical products, particularly medicines, need to be disposed of as waste as they are no longer effective or even fit for use (Ville de Goyet et al., 2012).

### *Medical Waste Management Plan*

Public health crises, such as Ebola and COVID-19, exposed flaws in the healthcare sector regarding the protocols and management for handling

*Table 3.7* Categories of Medical Waste

| *Category* | | *Description* |
|---|---|---|
| Hazardous Waste | Sharp Waste | • Items could cause cut or puncture wounds, for instance, needles, scalpels, and knives. |
| | Infectious Waste | • Items are suspected to contain sufficient amounts of pathogens, such as bacteria, viruses, parasites, and fungi, to cause diseases. Infectious waste is possibly generated from blood or other body fluids, cultures and stocks of infectious agents from laboratory work and waste from infected patients. |
| | Pathological Waste | • Items include tissues, organs, body parts, blood, body fluids, other waste from surgery, autopsies from infected patients, human foetuses, and infected animal carcasses. |
| | Pharmaceutical Waste | • Items include expired, unused, spilt and contaminated pharmaceutical products, prescribed and proprietary drugs, and vaccines, requiring careful disposal methods due to chemical or biological nature. |
| | Chemical Waste | • Items include discarded solid, liquid, and gaseous chemicals, which have the properties of toxicity, corrosiveness, flammability, reactivity, and oxidisation. |
| | Radioactive Waste | • Items are contaminated with radionuclides. |
| Non-hazardous | General Waste | • Items that have not interacted with infectious agents, hazardous chemicals or radioactive substances, which may pose sharp hazards, including cardboard boxes, paper, clear, coloured, or mixed glass. |

*Source*: WHO (2020)

medical waste, making medical waste sterilisation and disposal a highly material issue. Scholars stated that medical waste management practices are inherently poor due to ineffective policies, inadequate resources, and poor executions (Al-Khati et al., 2009; Babaee Tirkolaee & Aydın, 2021; Hossain et al., 2011; Longe, 2012; Lv et al., 2021). The WHO (2014) and Hicks (2013) state that the rising costs of medical wastage are caused by poor inventory management and overproduction due to demand overestimation. Correspondingly, poor medical waste management practices generate higher air emissions or black carbon emissions, creating adverse impacts on humans and the environment (Raila & Anderson, 2017).

Some medical technologies and measures provide the healthcare sector with the competency to sterilise medical waste on-site directly without excessively packaging the waste for transportation, reducing the likelihood of infection outbreaks and environmental impacts. Hence, Corse et al. (2015) suggest an on-site medical waste management system to improve the healthcare sector's ability for infectious waste containment and public protection, consisting of the process of responsibility assignment, waste generation assessment, plan development, implementation, monitoring, and training as described in Table 3.8 (Kandasamy et al., 2022; Tabash et al., 2016).

*Table 3.8* Medical Waste Management Plan

| *Process* | *Description* |
|---|---|
| Responsibility Assignment | • Nominate and create a waste management committee<br>• Assign duties and construct liaison arrangement |
| Waste Generation Assessment | • Identify the sources of medical waste<br>• Classify the types of medical waste based on applicable laws, policies and guidelines |
| Plan Development | • Estimate the quantities of generated waste, possibilities in waste minimisation, reuse, and recycling<br>• Identify and evaluate waste treatment and disposal treatment<br>• Consolidate medical waste management procedures based on the nature of each medical waste<br>• Outline monitoring procedures for waste categories and their destination |
| Implementation & Monitoring | • Execute medical waste collection, disposal and management, including thermal process, chemical process, and irradiation technologies<br>• Label medical waste with symbols accordingly to prevent health hazards during storage and transportation<br>• Conduct record-keeping and documentation<br>• Monitor onsite and offsite management performance<br>• Conduct third-party audit if necessary |
| Training | • Design and organise relevant training courses and programmes<br>• Educate relevant parties on proper medical waste handling and disposal |

*Source*: Kandasamy et al. (2022); Tabash et al. (2016)

### *Green Chemistry*

Given the increasing medical waste incineration, there is a need for waste reduction and therefore green chemistry in place to reduce waste and avoid wasteful production. Green chemistry refers to a pollution prevention initiative that dates back to the 1990s, consisting of 12 principles: (1) prevent waste generation in the beginning rather than treat or clean up waste after; (2) integrate synthetic methods to maximise the incorporation of all materials in the process into the final product; (3) design synthetic methodologies which use and generate sustention with little or no toxicity to human and environment if practicable; (4) preserve chemical efficacy and function while reducing toxicity; (5) limit the use of auxiliary substances when possible; (6) minimise the environmental and economic impacts of used energy if possible; (7) use renewable raw materials or feedstock; (8) reduce unnecessary derivatives; (9) use catalytic reagents rather than stoichiometric reagents if possible; (10) design chemical products to ensure at the end of their life cycle do not contaminate the ecosystem; (11) develop in-process monitoring and control system to enable real-time hazardous substances formation analysis; and (12) carefully select substances to minimise potential chemical accidents (Anastas & Warner, 1998).

Green chemistry advances the abilities of the healthcare sector against the challenges it faces in achieving sustainable consumption and production while delivering medical products and services for the better health of people. Green chemistry not only reduces waste generation through production but also minimises adverse impacts on the general public and the environment as summarised in Table 3.9 (EPA, 2023).

Together, medical waste management and green chemistry provide the healthcare sector the solutions for sustainable consumption and production, contributing to the following SDG 12 targets (Table 3.10).

*Table 3.9* Benefits of Green Chemistry

| *General Public* | *Environment* | *Economic* |
|---|---|---|
| • Fewer releases of hazardous air emissions and chemicals into the air<br>• Less discharge of hazardous wastewater and chemicals into water, leading to cleaner drinking water and recreational water<br>• Safer consumer products<br>• Less exposure to toxic chemicals<br>• Better population health | • Fewer releases of hazardous and toxic chemicals into the environment<br>• Lower potential for global warming, ozone depletion, and smog formation<br>• Less disruption of the ecosystem | • Lower production costs<br>• Higher productivity |

*Source*: EPA (2023)

*Table 3.10* Medical Waste Management and Green Chemistry and Associated SDG 12

| *Aspect* | *Associated SDG 12* |
|---|---|
| Medical Waste Management | • 12.4 By 2020, achieve the environmentally sound management of chemicals and all wastes throughout their life cycle, in accordance with agreed international frameworks, and significantly reduce their release to air, water, and soil in order to minimise their adverse impacts on human health and the environment |
| Green Chemistry | • 12.5 By 2030, substantially reduce waste generation through prevention, reduction, recycling, and reuse |

*Source*: The United Nations (2023a)

## Sustainable Stakeholder Engagement in Health Promotion Activities

Healthcare-related SDGs are heavily influenced by forces outside the healthcare sector, highlighting the interrelation and interconnections between stakeholders. The United Nations acknowledges that stakeholder engagement is crucial to drive progression, promote health, and develop innovative approaches, which should be dynamic and evolving, spanning sectors, industries and geographies, opening possible windows for all parties to act cohesively for better and creative solutions to improve health and well-being globally. Hence, SDG 17 attempts to demand governments to reinforce and achieve the implementation of the 17 SDGs and 169 targets together, including sufficient access to sciences, research and technology, funding and partnership.

In the context of healthcare promotion, SDG 17 encourages determination and implementation from the government to accelerate disease-tackling ability to safeguard the health, wellness, and welfare of the general public. Health promotion activities aim to safeguard patient welfare against counterfeit drugs and unethical marketing hype. Engagement and partnership at the country or regional level will cultivate the interaction, partnership and commitment at the sector and community level, addressing health disparities and inequality.

Progress to date, the United Nations estimates the world will not achieve SDGs by 2030. However, there is a strong demand for governments, industries, communities, and other sectors to collaborate and shape the future (The United Nations, 2023b). To facilitate SDG 17 regarding healthcare promotion, Figure 3.3 identifies associated stakeholders at each level and possible enabling methods for them to collaborate in the most productive ways.

### *At the Country Level*

In 2015, member countries of the United Nations answered a universal call to ensure healthier societies and the wellness of the populations at the global level. However, the "Leave no one behind" principle (The United

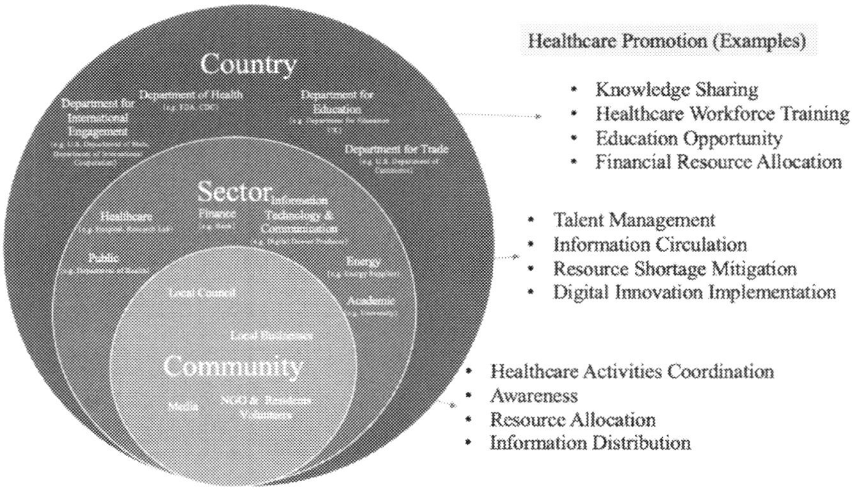


*Figure 3.3* Stakeholder Engagement for Health Promotion

*Source:* Authors

Nations, 2023b) is at significant risk. There are global imbalances in research and development, confronting the goals of making the production of healthcare-related sciences more inclusive and geographically diverse. Likewise, there are time lags between pioneering science, public policy, and implementation due to a lack of political will, lobbying, financial resources, and even disinformation. Countries realised the urgency of greater governmental engagements to accelerate health promotion globally and therefore integrate SDG 17 into existing legislation and framework. Evidence can be found in aspirations, new initiatives, and high-level development strategies; for instance, China incorporated the Goals in its 13th and 14th five-year plans and 2035 development targets and the African Union has linked the Goals with its Agenda 2063 (Research Institute for Eco-civilization, Chinese Academy for Social Science and United Nations Development Programme, 2022; The African Union, 2023).

Currently, governments have proactively advocated communication and cooperation to expand the accessibility of health promotion services about knowledge, innovation, and technology globally. Cross-country flows of capital, technology, and other resources have been widely observed to enhance synergies, remove trade-off barriers, and facilitate the healthcare development of another country. With the right enabling tools, the aforementioned flows can contribute to alleviating inequality and inaccessibility to healthcare services and advancing healthcare promotion. Table 3.11 summarises the possibilities of government engagement for health promotion

*Table 3.11* Health Promotion at the Country Level

| *Aspect* | | *Description* |
|---|---|---|
| Knowledge Sharing (innovation, technology, and data) | | • Stimulate international research and innovation, create co-lead R&D projects to strengthen the medical network and expand services and improve developing countries' capacities to absorb or adapt technology for health promotion<br>• Establish a joined medical task force to address periodic outreach or health crisis<br>• Create healthcare-related panels at the country level to bring together scientists, policymakers, and knowledge brokers to generate possible solutions accordingly and share knowledge openly as well as equitably |
| Healthcare Workforce Training | | • Educate and retrain healthcare workers to address staff shortage<br>• Assign elite healthcare professionals aboard |
| Education Opportunity | | • Sponsor foreign students to study abroad, expanding access to tertiary education and increasing their talent management in science, technology, and medical subjects |
| Financial Resources Allocation | Medical Products | • Donate medical products, such as vaccines, micronutrient supplementation for periodic outreach |
| | Funding | • Direct investment in healthcare projects in low-income countries to construct or reinforce medical infrastructure<br>• Taxes incentives and subsidiaries for medical export business or medical donation |

*Source*: Authors

globally (Markard et al., 2020; Stenberg et al., 2019; The United Nations, 2023b; UNESCO, 2021).

Engagement needs vary greatly among countries, but it shall follow these four pillars principally (Jones & Comfort, 2020; The United Nations, 2023b): (1) Strategic direction and foresight – all countries define strategies and steer action in line with SDGs and shared goals; (2) innovation and generation of new alternatives – developed countries should innovate, generate, and select suitable and sustainable alternatives, to scale and replicate solutions in developing countries to improve their competency in healthcare promotion; (3) impediment identification – all countries recognise unsustainable trajectories and reshape their mindset to foster political wellness and awareness for change; and (4) learning and resilience – all countries strengthen intuitions and networks through decentralisation, increasing diversity and redundancy of collaboration, monitoring, and continuous learning.

#### *At the Healthcare Sector Level*

The engagements at the country level encourage the industries to develop similar plans. Similarly, the need for effective engagement is increasing due to the complexity and inequality within the healthcare sector, demanding all parties to leverage their business strategies and business road maps, corporate sustainability programmes, public–private partnerships, and impact investing to increase access to healthcare and progressively aggregate healthcare development globally to align with SDGs. Notably, the healthcare sector and other related sectors have worked closely to solve four major challenges, namely talent management, information circulation, resource shortage mitigation, and digital innovation implementation. Table 3.12 captures the interrelationship of relevant sectors and summarises their engagement and contribution to healthcare promotions at the sector level.

#### *At the Community Level*

Stenberg et al. (2019) and GBD 2019 Under-5 Mortality Collaborators (2021) state the community should expand healthcare coverage and increase community-based partnerships or initiatives to optimise health promotion. Annan-Aggrey and Arku (2023) suggest the community should (1) identify and create locally owned, ambitious but achievable targets to sustain their engagement and participation in health promotion; and (2) enhance accountability through collaboration with local stakeholders, including leaders, citizens, and charity to jointly assess the progressions of health promotion (Esquivel & Sweetman, 2016). As such, the community ought to harness the skills and resources of local stakeholders to promote healthcare activities as summarised in Table 3.13 (Kasi, 2023).

Collectively, stakeholder engagement at the country level, sector level, and community level will contribute to SDG 17 as follows (The United Nations, 2023a):

- 17.9 Enhance international support for implementing effective and targeted capacity-building in developing countries to support national plans to implement all the SDGs, including through North–South, South–South, and triangular cooperation.
- 17.16 Enhance the Global Partnership for Sustainable Development, complemented by multi-stakeholder partnerships that mobilise and share knowledge, expertise, technology, and financial resources, to support the achievement of the SDGs in all countries, in particular developing countries.

### The Way Forward

The commonalities described earlier explicitly state the factors attributed to the fragility of the healthcare sector and health promotion, namely instability of energy infrastructure, innovation disruption, and sustainable consumption.

*Table 3.12* Engagement of Healthcare Sector for Health Promotion

| *Sector* | *Healthcare* | *Academic* | *Finance* | *Information Technology & Communication* | *Energy* | *Public* |
|---|---|---|---|---|---|---|
| Talent Management | √ | √ | | | | √ |
| | • Build partnerships with academic institutions for talent attraction, and continuing education opportunities to increase the quality of the workforce in the healthcare sector and ensure the performance of healthcare services<br>• Provide internships to students, allowing future healthcare professionals to gain primary insights into the sectors (PLOS Medicine Editors et al., 2016) | | | | | |
| Information Circulation | √ | | | √ | | √ |
| | • Simplify access to healthcare-related information and enable medical data sharing securely and safely to increase healthcare service efficiency<br>• Create anticounterfeit platforms to notify all stakeholders if counterfeit medicines have been reported and ensure the health and safety of the general public (World Bank, 2023a)<br>• Serialise and barcode packaging for traceability | | | | | |
| Resource Shortage Mitigation | √ | | √ | | √ | |
| | • Provide financial assistance to reinforce medical infrastructure, such as funding or donation, to improve medical capacities against overwhelming demands (Babatunde et al., 2019) | | | | | |
| Digital Innovation Implementation | √ | | | √ | | |
| | • Modernise R&D tools and equip the R&D team with innovative devices to remove barriers in medical research and shorten time for healthcare promotion (WHO, 2020) | | | | | |

*Source*: Babatunde et al. (2019); PLOS Medicine Editors et al. (2016); The World Bank (2023a)

*Table 3.13* Community Engagement for Health Promotion

| *Stakeholder* | *Examples* |
|---|---|
| Local Council | • Incorporate operations within the healthcare system to mitigate the wastage of money and materials<br>• Conduct regular events regarding diets, nutrition, and exercise to enhance participation and improve the utilisation of health-related infrastructure, products, and services |
| Non-governmental Organisation, Volunteers & Residents | • Advocate corporate sponsors and society representatives to work holistically for health promotion<br>• Raise awareness to promote health |
| Local Business | • Leverage goodwill and recourse to promote health at the community level |
| Media | • Distribute healthcare-related information<br>• Expand the reach and effectiveness of health promotion information |

*Source*: Authors

SDGs provide alternatives and solutions for the healthcare sector to enable continuity, stability, effective preparedness, and responses. Correspondingly, there are foreseeable trends regarding the sustainable development of the healthcare sector that improve robustness and resilience throughout the health crisis but also in the long term and in sustainable health promotion practices.

### *From Fragility to Resilience*

It is clear that the healthcare sector is under pressure to increase connectivity and resilience to deliver stable and seamless healthcare services in promoting health. Increasing pressures have stressed the healthcare sector to renew and reform its infrastructure for energy conservation in buildings, circularity in waste management, and maximising the application of digital technologies. Green energy may help overcome the fragility and vulnerability of the healthcare sector. Green energy integration provides lower-carbon alternatives for the healthcare sector to ensure the performance and productivity of healthcare services against the rising cost of fossil energy, instability of power supply, and stresses for carbon reduction. Digital innovation adds immense value to the healthcare sector in three main areas: (1) simplifying workflows and optimising effectiveness; (2) expanding medical accessibility and coverage to underserved areas; and (3) removing barriers for international R&D projects and shortening discover-to-market time. On the other hand, systematic medical waste management and green chemistry integration increase the resilience of the healthcare sector, which proactively complies with all applicable policies, regulations, and standards to ensure appropriate waste management and reduce waste generation from healthcare activities. Foreseeably, the pioneering development of energy, technology, and sciences will increase the resilience of the healthcare sector and advance public and community health by providing more stable and quality healthcare products and services.

### *From Inequity to Fairness and Accountability*

The COVID-19 pandemic has highlighted the profound facet of inequality in the global healthcare system, particularly when the demand for healthcare was growing heavily and rapidly. The healthcare-related resources were yet to be applied thoroughly to ensure fairness and accountability. August et al. (2022) suggest international and governmental engagements and partnerships regarding equitable health products and services. It is essential for all countries to coordinate and cooperate to eliminate inequality in accessibility. Besides, there is a need for international partnerships to identify possible optimal strategies for preparedness and management of future public health crises. Additionally, the principle of "leave no one behind" demands healthcare equity and accountability monitoring systems within countries, requiring resource aggregation to expand medical products and services to underserved areas and increase the feasibility of healthcare development globally (The United Nations, 2023b).

### *Implication for the Public Sector*

External changes may hinder the progression of sustainable development, arguing the imbalance, instability, and inequity of global healthcare. This chapter has paved the way for the public sector regarding the sustainable development of the healthcare sector. Accordingly, the public sector is encouraged to contribute to energy infrastructure reconstruction, digital innovation acceleration, sustainable consumption, and international engagement.

First, the public sector should increase investment in renewable energy infrastructure building and integrate renewable energy into the current energy mix to provide affordable, reliable, and lower-carbon energy to the industry and ultimately contribute to increasing renewable energy shares globally. Additionally, the public sector is encouraged to invest in and facilitate renewable energy research, increasing energy efficiency and advancing low-carbon energy development. Second, the rapid development of digital innovation acceleration has disrupted and revolutionised the healthcare sector. The public sector should actively encourage healthcare sectors to accelerate their digital integration to increase their performance and efficiency. Yet, highly digital integration raises issues regarding data privacy and cybersecurity. The public sector should redirect its focus to ensure the integrity of data collection, aggregation and sharing, and safeguard the rights of the data providers. Third, for sustainable consumption and production, the healthcare sector generates medical waste throughout the lifecycle of delivering medical services, resulting in adverse impacts on the environment, human population and society. Therefore, the public sector should create waste management regulations, policies, and guidance in accordance with internationally accepted frameworks and encourage the healthcare sector to uphold the "Reuse, Recycle and Reduce" principles to minimise waste generation. Fourth, the public sector should participate in international engagement, coordination, and partnership to share knowledge, expertise, technology, and resources to support and increase the capacity-building of the global healthcare system in sustainable health promotion practices for the benefit of mankind.

### *Implication for the Private Sector*

Megatrends, particularly climate change, resource scarcity, and technological breakthroughs, are exponentially increasing the scope, speed and interrelatedness of challenges of health promotion. Critical issues such as energy instability and technological breakthroughs demand timely attention from the private sector to accelerate the quality and performance of health promotion. Unfortunately, the healthcare sector mainly develops partnerships within the sector itself to address the problems at the scale at which they exist. Every sector is involved in health promotion acceleration, and hence, cross-sector partnerships are highly encouraged, including partnerships between public-sector companies and social service organisations or between private companies and healthcare research institutions to promote health.

First, the healthcare sector should identify the current issues in health promotion acceleration and seek potential solutions across sectors to interact and collaborate with multiple stakeholders to create solutions jointly and contribute to SDGs adequately. Second, the private sectors ought to minimise differences and disagreements to develop a shared vision in health promotion practices. Third, private sectors should leverage resources as well as share expertise and knowledge together to amplify the impact and results of health promotion.

## References

Adair-Rohani, H., Zukor, K., Bonjour, S., Wilburn, S., Kuesel, A., Hebert, R., & Fletcher, E. (2013). Limited electricity access in health facilities of sub-Saharan Africa: A systematic review of data on electricity access, sources, and reliability. *Global Health Science and Practice*, *1*(2), 249–261. https://doi.org/10.9745/GHSP-D-13-00037

The African Union. (2023). *Agenda 2063: The Africa we want*. The African Union Commission. Retrieved November 27, 2023, from https://au.int/en/agenda2063/overview

Akinyele, D. O. (2017). Techno-economic design and performance analysis of nanogrid systems for households in energy-poor villages. *Sustainable Cities and Society*, *34*, 335–357. https://doi.org/10.1016/j.scs.2017.07.004

Akinyele, D. O., Rayudu, R. K., & Tan, R. H. G. (2016). Comparative study of photovoltaic technologies based on performance, cost and space requirement: Strategy for selection and application. *International Journal of Green Energy*, *13*(13), 1352–1368. https://doi.org/10.1080/15435075.2015.1112287

Al-Khati, I., Al-Qaroot, Y., & Ali-Shtayeh, M. (2009). Management of healthcare waste in circumstances of limited resources: A case study in the hospitals of Nablus city-Palestine. *Waste Management & Research*, *27*, 305–312. https://doi.org/10.1177/0734242X08094124

Amankwah-Amoah, J. (2020). Note: Mayday, mayday, mayday! Responding to environmental shocks: Insights on global airlines' responses to COVID-19.

*Transportation Research Part E: Logistics and Transportation Review, 143*. https://doi.org/10.1016/j.tre.2020.102098

Anastas, P. T., & Warner, J. C. (1998). *Green chemistry: Theory and practice*. Oxford University Press.

Annan-Aggrey, E., & Arku, G. (2023). 'New wine in old wineskins?' – Understanding the framing of SDGs in the local government context in Ghana. *Progress in Development Studies, 23*(3), 229–245. https://doi.org/10.1177/14649934231182538

Asongu, S. A., Diop, S., & Nnanna, J. (2020). Health vulnerability versus economic resilience to the COVID-19 pandemic: Global evidence. *World Affairs, 184*(4), 472–500. https://doi.org/10.1177/00438200211052045

August, E., Tadesse, L., O'Neill, M., Eisenberg, J., Wong, R., Kolars, J., & Bekele, A. (2022). What is global health equity? A proposed definition. *Annals of Global Health, 88*(1), 50. https://doi.org/10.5334/aogh.3754

Babaee Tirkolaee, E., & Aydın, N. S. (2021). A sustainable medical waste collection and transportation model for pandemics. *Waste Management & Research, 39*, 34–44. https://doi.org/10.1177/0734242X211000437

Babatunde, O., Adedoja, O., Babatunde, D., & Denwigwe, I. (2019). Off-grid hybrid renewable energy system for rural healthcare centers: A case study in Nigeria. *Energy Science & Engineering, 7*, 676–693. https://doi.org/10.1002/ese3.314

Baudier, P., Kondrateva, G., Ammi, C., Chang, V., & Schiavone, F. (2023). Digital transformation of healthcare during the COVID-19 pandemic: Patients' teleconsultation acceptance and trusting beliefs. *Technovation, 120*(2023), 102547. https://doi.org/10.1016/j.technovation.2022.102547

Biogen. (2023). *2022 ESG report*. Retrieved November 27, 2023, from www.biogen.com/content/dam/corporate/international/global/en-US/docs/esg-report/2022-ESG-Report.pdf

Borzuei, D., Moosavian, S. F., & Ahmadi, A. (2022). Investigating the dependence of energy prices and economic growth rates with emphasis on the development of renewable energy for sustainable development in Iran. *Sustainable Development, 30*, 848–854. https://doi.org/10.1002/sd.2284

Budd, J., Miller, B., Manning, E., Lampos, V., Zhuang, M., Edelstein, M., & Rees, G. (2020). Digital technologies in the public-health response to COVID-19. *Nature Medicine, 26*(8), 1183–1192. https://doi.org/10.1038/s41591-020-1011-4

Corse, T., Thomas, K., Broderick, J., Kabiri, N. S., Margulies, J., Masri, T., McCullen, J., & McMahon, M. (2015). Using Ebola as a lens to examine medical waste sterilization. *World Medical & Health Policy, 7*, 402–411. https://doi.org/10.1002/wmh3.164

Costanza, R., Fioramonti, L., & Kubiszewski, I. (2016). The UN sustainable development goals and the dynamics of well-being. *Frontiers in Ecology and the Environment, 14*(2), 59–59. https://doi.org/10.1002/fee.1231

Costello, A., Abbas, M., Allen, A., Ball, S., Bell, S., Bellamy, R., Friel, S., Groce, N., Johnson, A., Kett, M., Lee, M., Levy, C., Maslin, M., McCoy, D., McGuire, B., Montgomery, H., Napier, D., Pagel, C., Patel, J., & Patterson, C. (2009). Managing the health effects of climate change: Lancet and University College London Institute for Global Health Commission. *Lancet, 373*(9676), 1673–1733. https://doi.org/10.1016/S0140-6736(09)60935-1

Dawkins, B., Renwick, C., Ensor, T., Shinkins, B., Jayne, D., & Meads, D. (2021). What factors affect patients' ability to access healthcare? An overview of systematic reviews. *Tropical Medicine & International Health, 26*, 1177–1188. https://doi.org/10.1111/tmi.13651

Diop, S., Asongu, S. A., & Nnanna, J. (2020). COVID-19 economic vulnerability and resilience indexes: Global evidence. *International Social Science Journal, 71*(S1), 37–50. https://doi.org/10.1111/issj.12276

Doherty, A., Wall, A., Khaldi, N., & Kussmann, M. (2021). Artificial intelligence in functional food ingredient discovery and characterisation: A focus on bioactive plant and food peptides. *Frontiers in Genetics*, *12*, 768979. https://doi.org/10.3389/fgene.2021.768979

Dufo-Lópeza, R., Pérez-Cebolladaa, E., Bernal-Agustína, J., & Martínez-Ruizb, I. (2016). Optimisation of energy supply at off-grid healthcare facilities using Monte Carlo simulation. *Energy Conversion and Management*, *113*, 321–330. https://doi.org/10.1016/j.enconman.2016.11.057

EPA. (2023, May 9). *Benefits of green chemistry*. Retrieved November 25, 2023, from www.epa.gov/greenchemistry/benefits-green-chemistry#:~:text=Green%20chemicals%20either%20degrade%20to,Less%20chemical%20disruption%20of%20ecosystems

Esquivel, V., & Sweetman, C. (2016). Gender and the sustainable development goals. *Gender & Development*, *24*(1), 1–8. https://doi.org/10.1080/13552074.2016.1153318

Gasper, D., Shah, A., & Tankha, S. (2019). The framing of sustainable consumption and production in SDG 12. *Global Policy*, *10*(S1), 83–95. https://doi.org/10.1111/1758-5899.12592

GBD 2019 Under-5 Mortality Collaborators. (2021). Global, regional, and national progress towards Sustainable Development Goal 3.2 for neonatal and child health: All-cause and cause-specific mortality findings from the Global Burden of Disease Study 2019. *Lancet*, *398*(10303), 870–905. https://doi.org/10.1016/S0140-6736(21)01207-1

Golinelli, D., Boetto, E., Carullo, G., Nuzzolese, A., Landini, M., & Fantini, M. (2020). Adoption of digital technologies in health care during the COVID-19 pandemic: Systematic review of early scientific literature. *Journal of Medical Internet Research*, *22*(11), e22280. https://doi.org/10.2196/22280

Heinrichs, H., Mueller, F., Rohfleisch, L., Schulz, V., Talbot, S., & Kiessling, F. (2022). Digitalization impacts the COVID-19 pandemic and the stringency of government measures. *Scientific Reports*, *12*(1), 21628. https://doi.org/10.1038/s41598-022-24726-0

Hicks, R. (2013). *An exploration of healthcare inventory and lean management in minimizing medical supply waste in healthcare organizations* (Publication Number 2013. 3558365). Walden University. www.proquest.com/docview/1350640333

Hossain, M., Santhanam, A., Norulaini, N., & Omar, A. (2011). Clinical solid waste management practices and its impact on human health and environment– A review. *Waste Management*, *31*(4), 754–766. https://doi.org/10.1016/j.wasman.2010.11.008

Ibisch, P. L., Hoffmann, M. T., Kreft, S., Pe'er, G., Kati, V., Biber-Freudenberger, L., DellaSala, D. A., Vale, M. M., Hobson, P. R., & Selva, N. (2016). A global map of roadless areas and their conservation status. *Science*, *354*(6318), 1423–1427. https://doi.org/10.1126/science.aaf7166

IQVIA. (2023). *IQVIA 2022 ESG report*. Retrieved November 27, 2023, from www.iqvia.com/-/media/iqvia/pdfs/about-us/esg/iqvia-2022-esg-report.pdf

Jones, P., & Comfort, D. (2020). A commentary on the localisation of the sustainable development goals. *Journal of Public Affairs*, *20*(1), e1943. https://doi.org/10.1002/pa.1943

Kandasamy, J., Kinare, Y. P., Pawar, M. T., Majumdar, A., K. E. K., V., & Agrawal, R. (2022). Circular economy adoption challenges in medical waste management for sustainable development: An empirical study. *Sustainable Development*, *30*(5), 958–975. https://doi.org/10.1002/sd.2293

Kasi, S. (2023). A new strategy for rejuvenating primary healthcare: The government-society partnership model. *Journal of Primary Care & Community Health*, *14*, 1–7. https://doi.org/10.1177/21501319231200763

Lancet, T. (2009). A commission on climate change. *Lancet*, *373*(9676), 1659.

Leung, T. C. H., Chiu, W. K., You, S. X., & Fong, B. Y. F. (2023). *ESG and sustainable development in healthcare*. Springer.

Longe, E. (2012). Healthcare waste management status in Lagos State, Nigeria: A case study from selected healthcare facilities in Ikorodu and Lagos metropolis. *Waste Management & Research*, *30*, 562–571. https://doi.org/10.1177/0734242X11412109

Lv, J., Yang, J., Xue, J., Zhu, P., Liu, L., & Li, S. (2021). Investigation of potential safety hazards during medical waste disposal in SARS-CoV-2 testing laboratory. *Environmental Science and Pollution Research*, *28*(7), 35822–35829. https://doi.org/10.1007/s11356-021-13247-4

Markard, J., Geels, F., & Raven, R. (2020). Challenges in the acceleration of sustainability transitions. *Environmental Research Letters*, *15*(8), 081001.

MSCI. (2023). *ESG industry materiality map*. Retrieved November 11, 2023, from www.msci.com/our-solutions/esg-investing/esg-industry-materiality-map

Osei-Frimpong, K., Wilson, A., & Owusu-Frimpong, N. (2015). Service experiences and dyadic value co-creation in healthcare service delivery: A CIT approach. *Journal of Service Theory and Practice*, *25*(4), 443–462. https://doi.org/10.1108/JSTP-03-2014-0062

Paul, D., Sanap, G., Shenoy, S., Kalyane, D., Kalia, K., & Tekade, R. (2020). Artificial intelligence in drug discovery and development. *Drug Discovery Today*, *26*(1), 80–93. https://doi.org/10.1016/j.drudis.2020.10.010

Perera, A. T. D., Wickramasinghe, P. U., Nik, V. M., & Scartezzini, J. L. (2019). Machine learning methods to assist energy system optimization. *Applied Energy*, *243*, 191–205. https://doi.org/10.1016/j.apenergy.2019.03.202

PLOS Medicine Editors, Rid, A., Johansson, M., Leung, G., Valantine, H., Burchard, E., Oh, S., & Zimmerman, C. (2016). Towards equity in health: Researchers take stock. *PLoS Medicine*, *13*(11), e1002186. https://doi.org/10.1371/journal.pmed.1002186

Raila, E., & Anderson, D. (2017). Healthcare waste management during disasters and its effects on climate change: Lessons from 2010 earthquake and cholera tragedies in Haiti. *Waste Management & Research*, *35*(3), 236–245. https://doi.org/10.1177/0734242X16682312

Research Institute for Eco-civilization Chinese Academy for Social Science United Nations Development Programme. (2022). *Shenzhen sustainable development report 2021*. www.undp.org/sites/g/files/zskgke326/files/2022-05/UNDP-CH-EN-Shenzen%20Sustainable%20Development%20Report-2021.pdf

Rickels, W., Dovern, J., Hoffmann, J., Quaas, M. F., Schmidt, J. O., & Visbeck, M. (2016). Indicators for monitoring sustainable development goals: An application to oceanic development in the European Union. *Earth's Future*, *4*(5), 252–267. https://doi.org/10.1002/2016EF000353

Romero, I., & Carnero, M. C. (2019). Environmental assessment in health care organizations. *Environmental Science and Pollution Research*, *26*(4), 3196–3207. https://doi.org/10.1007/s11356-017-1016-9

Sachs, J., Schmidt-Traub, G., Kroll, C., Durand-Delacre, D., & Teksoz, K. (2017). *SDG index and dashboards report*. Bertelsmann Stiftung and Sustainable Development Solutions Network (SDSN).

Schmidheiny, S. (1992). *Changing course: A global business perspective on development and the environment*. MIT Press.

Schmidt, H., Gostin, L., & Emanuel, E. (2015). Public health, universal health coverage, and sustainable development goals: Can they coexist? *Lancet*, *386*(9996), 928–930. https://doi.org/10.1016/S0140-6736(15)60244-6

Siciliano, G., Wallbott, L., Urban, F., Dang, A. N., & Lederer, M. (2021). Low-carbon energy, sustainable development, and justice: Towards a just energy transition for the society and the environment. *Sustainable Development*, *29*(6), 1049–1061. https://doi.org/10.1002/sd.2193

Slater, M., & Bartlett, S. (2023). Climate change: What healthcare professionals can do. *Journal of the Royal College of Physicians of Edinburgh*, *53*(1), 7–8. https://doi.org/10.1177/14782715231158878

S&P. (2023, November 11). *GICS: Global industry classification standard*. www.spglobal.com/spdji/en/landing/topic/gics/

Stenberg, K., Hanssen, O., Bertram, M., Brindley, C., Meshreky, A., Barkley, S., & Tan-Torres Edejer, T. (2019). Guide posts for investment in primary health care and projected resource needs in 67 low-income and middle-income countries: A modelling study. *Lancet Global Health*, *7*(11), e1500–e1510. https://doi.org/10.1016/S2214-109X(19)30416-4

Tabash, M. I., Hussein, R. A., Mahmoud, A. H., El-Borgy, M. D., & Abu-Hamad, B. A. (2016). Impact of an educational program on knowledge and practice of health care staff toward pharmaceutical waste management in Gaza, Palestine. *Journal of the Air and Waste Management Association*, *66*(4), 429–438. https://doi.org/10.1080/10962247.2016.1146638

UNESCO. (2021). *UNESCO recommendation on open science*. https://unesdoc.unesco.org/ark:/48223/pf0000379949

The United Nations. (2002). *Plan of implementation of the world summit on sustainable development*. https://documents-dds-ny.un.org/doc/UNDOC/GEN/N02/636/93/PDF/N0263693.pdf?OpenElement

The United Nations. (2015). *Transforming our world: The 2030 agenda for sustainable development*. www.un.org/ga/search/view_doc.asp?symbol=A/RES/70/1&Lang=E

The United Nations. (2023a). *The 17 goals*. Retrieved November 27, 2023, from https://sdgs.un.org/goals

The United Nations. (2023b). *Global sustainable development report 2023: Times of crisis, times of change: Science for accelerating transformations to sustainable development*. https://sdgs.un.org/sites/default/files/2023-09/FINAL%20GSDR%202023-Digital%20-110923_1.pdf

Vallathan, G., Meyyappan, S., & Rajani, T. (2022). Healthcare: Energy optimization techniques using IoT and machine learning. In A. John, S. Mohan, S. Padmanaban, & Y. Hamid (Eds.), *Hybrid intelligent approaches for smart energy: Practical applications*. https://doi.org/10.1002/9781119821878.ch14

Ville de Goyet, C., Sarmiento, J., & Grünewald, F. (2012). *Health response to the earthquake in Haiti January 2010 Lessons to be learned for the next massive sudden-onset disaster*. Pan American Health Organization.

Vohra, K., Vodonos, A., Schwartz, J., Marais, E., Sulprizio, M., & Mickley, L. (2021). Global mortality from outdoor fine particle pollution generated by fossil fuel combustion: Results from GEOS-Chem. *Environmental Research*, *195*(110754). https://doi.org/10.1016/j.envres.2021.110754

Wei, Y., Cui, M., Ye, Z., & Guo, Q. (2021). Environmental challenges from the increasing medical waste since SARS outbreak. *Journal of Cleaner Production*, *291*, 125246. https://doi.org/10.1016/j.jclepro.2020.125246

WHO. (2014). *Safe management of wastes from health-care activities* (2nd ed.). https://iris.who.int/bitstream/handle/10665/85349/9789241548564_eng.pdf?sequence=1

WHO. (2020). *Digital health implementation investment guide (DIIG): Integrating digital interventions into health programmes*. https://iris.who.int/bitstream/handle/10665/334306/9789240010567-eng.pdf?sequence=1

Wong, C., Siah, K., & Lo, A. (2019). Estimation of clinical trial success rates and related parameters. *Biostatistics*, *20*(2), 273–286. https://doi.org/10.1093/biostatistics/kxx069

The World Bank. (2023a). *Digital-in-health: Unlocking the value for everyone*. www.worldbank.org/en/topic/health/publication/digital-in-health-unlocking-the-value-for-everyone

The World Bank. (2023b). *Health and climate change*. Retrieved November 14, 2023, from www.worldbank.org/en/topic/health/brief/health-and-climate-change

Xiong, S., Lu, H., Peoples, N., Duman, E., Najarro, A., Ni, Z., Gong, E., Yin, R., Ostbye, T., Palileo-Villanueva, L., Doma, R., Kafle, S., Tian, M., & Yan, L. (2023). Digital health interventions for non-communicable disease management in primary health care in low-and middle-income countries. *NPJ Digital Medicine*, *12*. https://doi.org/10.1038/s41746-023-00764-4

# 4 Environmental and Ecological Determinants and Population Health

*Sherry Fung and Wang-Kin Chiu*

## Introduction

One of the concepts of economics simply defines and mentions that human wants are unlimited, whether material or non-material. Among the possibilities of human desire, health is one of the most desired goals or purposes of life for all people. Everyone wishes and needs good health and well-being. Everyone has the right to good health. People would usually consider health issues as personal matters with top priority – "Without health, there is nothing in life". The health of a community or population, as well as the health of an individual, is equally important to everyone as every person is living and being closely involved in the community. Population health is an essential approach to assess health outcomes and drive improvements for a group of individuals, who can be affected in various ways. In particular, population health is continuously affected considerably by the environment and ecology, which may be altered by human activities, and so, humans, the environment and population health are interrelated. Health for all is of the utmost importance. It is therefore no surprise that transformative and systems approaches to achieving and promoting health for all have been strongly advocated (Fong & Chiu, 2023).

Health is not only one of the targets; it is one of the basic conditions for living and is pursued by every individual. There are several organisations and volunteers that contribute to constructing healthcare systems, providing healthcare services, and promoting different health-related information, including disease prevention, lifestyle and risk management, health promotion, and so on. For example, the United Nations (UN) planned and initiated the 2030 Agenda for Sustainable Development in 2015. It aims to build a desirable, secure, and prosperous world by applying the revolutionary concept of sustainable development and setting 17 Sustainable Development Goals (SDGs). All SDGs describe and provide different dimensions to achieve sustainable development, such as SDG 3 which expresses the clear goal of health for all by ensuring a healthy life and promoting well-being (The Global Goals, n.d.).

It is believed that the proposed framework is a plan with strategies. Ideally, the framework would be followed and implemented to achieve the goals. Unfortunately, things seldom work out as planned; sometimes problems and

DOI: 10.4324/9781032701356-4

issues arise during the implementation of different measures according to the plan. In recent years, the real situation has gone off-track, especially when the outbreak of coronavirus disease 2019 (COVID-19) infection has created serious global impacts. There is no denying that COVID-19 has wreaked havoc across the globe and become a major obstacle that could prevent the world from achieving its goals. The critical underlying issues that evolved in the pandemic are putting the globe at risk.

There are two sides to every coin. However, a crisis may be turned into an opportunity. After a long fight against the COVID-19 virus, the post-pandemic era beckons, everyone is now moving forward, resuming, and returning to normal life. Time has changed, and the world has also changed. Many things have undergone changes in countless ways. After the pandemic, the designated framework will need to be reviewed and amended to adapt to the accelerated pace of change in the world, which may be faster than we can imagine.

The environmental and ecological determinants of health will be discussed in this chapter, and the current understanding of how critical health issues have altered the environment and ecosystems, which have also affected the global economy and the fulfilment of the health-related SDGs, will also be explored.

## Environmental and Ecological Determinants of Health

Health is a huge topic of broad and current interest to the governments, healthcare professionals, academia, and the general public because it reflects the overall status of physical, mental, and social well-being of an individual as well as a community. Unlike other health topics, population health is currently not uniformly defined by any influential global health-related committee or organisation. The most common definition of population health was proposed and provided by Kindig and Stoddart (2003), who defined it as the health outcomes of a group of people. The grouping of population is not defined, but rather by clustering and studying the states and behaviours of different groups of people, such as geographic regions, state dynamics, education level, race, ethnicity, indigenousness, gender, and whatnot. The Centers for Medicare and Medicaid Services has further elaborated on the definition of population health which links with the effect of contextual factors within the group (The Centers for Medicare and Medicaid Services, 2023). Instead of focusing on the health of an individual, it would be encouraged to recognise the needs and then take targeted measures to achieve the health-related goals which each individual craves by taking into account and assessing the overall health of the specific population or most communities.

There are many factors that determine health. In addition to the social and economic determinants discussed in previous chapters, environmental, and ecological determinants play a vital role in enhancing population health. Simply, the air we breathe, the water we drink, the food we eat, and everything we need and use come from nature and the surrounding environment. The health of people cannot be fulfilled without the support of the environment and ecosystems, and therefore, a sustainable environment is crucial for us to significantly contribute to and positively impact population health. A green and clean environment is in particular significant to the attainment of sustainable health, with due consideration of the growing ageing population around the world and vulnerability of the population group to a high level of contaminants in the environment (Chiu & Fong, 2022). The interplay between the environment, population health, and sustainable development is a complex and dynamic relationship. The environmental and ecological determinants of health influence the globe to a great extent, and the SDGs provide a comprehensive framework for addressing global challenges, including those related to health and the environment.

### *Food Security*

Food is a major need and necessity to sustain life for all. Through the intake of food, people receive well-balanced nutrition and convert it into energy for body functions and body tissues for promoting physical health and growth. People can obtain both plant-based and animal-based food, ultimately to be served on the plate from the natural environment. Different kinds of foods are then further produced and processed on the basis of raw ingredients and materials. Access to a sufficient quantity and quality of nutritious food is fundamental to human existence. Food security is defined as the state in which all individuals are available and have access to sufficient, safe, and nutritious food to fulfil dietary needs and preferences with four dimensions simultaneously, including availability, access, utilisation, and stability (The World Bank Group, n.d.).

While everyone needs food, some people face hunger or malnutrition because their access to food is limited and insecure, and the lack of consistent access to adequate food is a violation of food security. In particular, for heavily populated countries, food security has been a top agenda among the major public health issues (Lam et al., 2013). The Food and Agriculture Organization of the UN reported that about 691 million to 783 million people in the world faced hunger in 2022 (Food and Agriculture Organization of the United Nations, n.d.). The news and announcements often report that people living in lower-income and developing countries, such as Afghanistan, Ethiopia, the Democratic Republic of Congo, Syria, Yemen, and so forth, are experiencing food insecurity (Central Intelligence Agency, n.d.; The Economist Impact, n.d.; World Food Program USA, 2023). In fact, people living in developed countries are also affected by food insecurity due to several factors. For instance, Tarasuk et al. (2019) examined the situation in Canada and found that the severity of Canadian food insecurity is varied by geographic residence and other social variables. Dhunna and Tarasuk (2021) also found out that the Black population in Canada is more susceptible to food insecurity because of their racialised identity.

The suffering populations are more likely to have poorer health. Firstly, food security affects physical health with diet quality and nutrient intake. It is believed that people experiencing food insecurity either are malnourished and have difficulty accessing nutritious food or overnourished and are at risk of chronic diseases due to excessive intake of processed and unhealthy food ("Food Insecurity: A Public Health Issue", 2016), leading to the situation that they could not gain beneficial nutritional status and fulfil the food utilisation dimension. Secondly, food insecurity has a significant effect on mental health. According to Pourmotabbed et al. (2020), food insecurity is positively associated with depression and stress, as the concern about food availability and access increases the risk of experiencing symptoms of a mental health disorder. As a result, health cannot be guaranteed or maintained in a situation of food insecurity.

Since the impacts on population health and sustainable development constitute a chain of consequences, starting from environmental degradation and ending with food insecurity, the UN has recognised the importance of food security in order to make people able to live without hunger and to promote sustainable agricultural production, all of which are encapsulated in SDG 2 (The United Nations, n.d.). Pérez-Escamilla (2017) has concluded that food security has an impact on human beings from physical, social, and environmental perspectives, namely child development, risk of disease, social unrest, and whatnot, which is linked to SDG 2 and even the remaining SDGs. Therefore, food security is important to maintain the health and well-being of individuals and communities and support sustainable development.

### *Water and Sanitation*

As everyone knows, water is the basis of all life on Earth. It is believed that water is crucial to every living being because it is the initial source of development and creation of major civilisations in the world. In ancient religions and mythology, deities associated with water, such as the ancient Greek myth of Oceanus, the ancient Egyptian god Nu (or Nun), and the Bugkalot god of the life-giving water (rain), Oden, emphasised the significance of and connection between water and life through embodied and personified images. Apart from symbolic meaning in religious creation myths, water is purely an important and prime source of life. Indeed, water is at the core of life for the health and survival of living organisms. Water is indispensable for daily living and production, and it is also involved in the functioning reactions of living organisms and the climate system.

Access to safe water with adequate sanitation is also one of the human rights and is necessary for maintaining good health through building physical health and preventing waterborne diseases. Yet there are still people in the world who cannot obtain clean and safe water, along with basic sanitation services. United Nations Children's Fund (UNICEF) (2023) has reported that around 2.2 billion (one-third of the global population) and 3.5 billion (half of the global population) people will be unable to access satisfactory water and managed sanitation services, respectively, in 2022. These people are facing the profound consequences of inadequate water and sanitation. Population health will be directly affected by a substantial disease burden due to the lack of quality water and sanitation. Without clean and safe water, the risk of getting life-threatening waterborne diseases, such as cholera, diarrhoea, dysentery, hepatitis A, typhoid, and polio, rises, especially among vulnerable populations (World Health Organization [WHO], 2023a).

Furthermore, the UN has explicitly recognised the importance of water and sanitation in SDG 6 (Department of Economic and Social Affairs, The United Nations, n.d.). The availability and coverage of clean water and basic sanitation are as essential as basic services that are accessible to all and connected to wastewater treatment. The significance and expected impacts of achieving the Targets of SDG 6 have been elaborated (Arora & Mishra, 2022; Howard, 2021). The most direct impact is on physical health, which is what Target 6.1 aims to achieve. Besides, water quality management and wastewater treatment contribute to improved sanitation and hygiene (Target 6.2), thereby further reducing antimicrobial resistance (Target 6.3). Otherwise, unqualified water may harm health, daily living, agricultural production, and wastewater disposal.

It is obvious that this life-sustaining need has to be fulfilled by solving water and sanitation management and inequality. Water and sanitation, as a key environmental determinant, directly impacts population health and supports sustainable development. Ensuring the availability and safe water through proper water treatment and infrastructure development, as well as the promotion of sanitation and hygiene practices, can significantly improve population health through the prevention of waterborne diseases and associated health risks and further advance the fulfilment of SDGs.

### *Energy Access*

In modern society, people use a lot of machinery and consume a lot of energy. Energy can be obtained from many forms of resources, categorised generally as renewable energy and non-renewable energy. As stated by the U.S. Energy Information Administration (2023), renewable or green energy sources include solar energy, wind energy, hydropower, geothermal energy, and bioenergy (or known as biomass); and non-renewable energy sources include fossil fuels (coal, petroleum, and natural gas), hydrocarbon gas liquids, and nuclear energy. By taking energy from raw energy sources, it can be transformed or converted into different forms of energy to be utilised, of which electrical energy (electricity) converted is widely used today.

Electricity is as important as food and water in modern daily life, from lighting to powering the life-saving medical equipment in healthcare facilities, demonstrating that access to energy is a key environmental determinant of health, with profound impacts on population health, well-being, and socio-economic development outcomes. Nevertheless, the International Energy Agency (2023) projected that around 760 million people in the world will not have access to energy in 2022. Besides, it is estimated that one of the global challenges to health is that approximately 1 billion people do not obtain access to healthcare services with stable energy sources (WHO, 2023c).

Lack of or poor access to energy is a major obstacle to achieving health. Porcaro et al. (2017) summarised the uses and benefits of electrification in healthcare facilities, in terms of replacing and adopting modern electrically driven energy technologies or processes, for example, providing minimal lighting and power to support more successful child deliveries and to reduce complications associated with pregnancy and childbirth; improving the ability of refrigerating vaccines, blood, and medicines to prevent and control disease; enabling communication and IT services to enhance outreach and education using telemedicine or e-health and so forth. It is undeniable that energy plays a vital role in facilitating health services.

Besides, energy is a key to support daily living and various human activities such as agriculture, commerce, production, transportation, and education. Therefore, a clean, reliable, and affordable energy access, a focus of SDG 7, is equally important and essential to health and sustainable development. In addition to the electrification of healthcare facilities, an affordable, reliable, and sustainable energy access could also contribute to maximising social benefits and infrastructures (Fuso Nerini et al., 2018). People can benefit from accessing a number of basic services and improving their livelihoods. Take education as an example, people can both acquire adequate knowledge and skills in energy supply-supported educational facilities and receive information to deepen their understanding of the communities and even gain vision for national and global developments. There has also been a surging amount of studies reporting the use of various electrical facilities and emerging technologies in contemporary education during the new era of digitalisation and artificial intelligence (Chiu, 2021). Relevant innovations and applications in educational settings have been investigated with the important goal of nurturing responsible citizens and moving the society towards a sustainable environment. Examples can be found in the teaching and learning of specific subjects, including those in the discipline of environmental science. All these support and demonstrate that energy access is critical to the achievement of the relevant SDGs.

Therefore, it is desirable to use sustainable energy sources instead of traditional or non-renewable energy sources nowadays. The adoption of sustainable energy resources and the management of natural resources in a way that meets the needs of the present generation will help to preserve the environment and ecosystems for future generations, ensure a continuous supply and availability of energy resources, and ultimately improve population health.

### *Climate Change*

Climate is defined as the overall weather pattern of a region or an area over a long period of time (World Meteorological Organization [WMO], n.d.), regulated by the complex interactions between different components of the Earth and the atmospheric, oceanic, geological, and biological systems. In nature, the Earth's climate is constantly changing and fluctuating. In accordance with Climate Science Investigations (2023), there are different natural causes, namely changes in the Earth's orbit, volcanic eruptions, variations in solar activity, and tectonic shifts, all of which affect the planetary climate. It is undeniable that the Earth is vital to support and sustain life, and life on the planet depends on and is influenced by the climate. The behaviour of life affects the climate system, and in turn, climate change indicates where and how species are surviving.

In addition, recent climate change is caused and explained by historical developments (Driga & Drigas, 2019). Since the Industrial Revolution in the eighteenth century, increased human activities and greenhouse gas emissions have led to global warming and altered the climate of this planet. However, the acceleration of climate change by unnatural processes has become the major challenge of our times. Climate change affects health through various pathways and mechanisms, and poses significant health risks such as extreme weather events, heat-related illnesses, food and water insecurity, and other problems, reflecting that the basic elements supporting good health and life are threatened. As described by Ebi et al. (2021), it is increasingly recognised that climate change will lead to more untoward consequences and further development of risks to population health, including increasingly raised levels of air pollution, heat wave-related morbidity and mortality, occupational health and safety hazards associated with exposure to high temperatures and hot environments, more frequent and severe natural extreme events and disasters, such as droughts, floods, and wildfires, and the potential of vector-borne disease infections. In addition, human activities exacerbate climate change and health issues, leading to environmental degradation, loss of biodiversity and psychological health issues following extreme weather events (Agache et al., 2022). Therefore, climate change is visibly affecting the environment and ecosystems which in turn poses challenges to global health.

Moreover, the effects of climate change on the environment and health are emphasised in several SDGs as climate change is both a consequence and a driver of sustainable development. The UN has noticed the crisis arising from extreme climate change and called for urgent actions under SDG 13 (The United Nations Environment Programme, n.d.). Fuso Nerini et al. (2019) have emphasised that SDG 13 is interlinked with other SDGs, highlighting the need for an integrated approach to sustainable development. In general, addressing climate change contributes to the achievement of SDGs 2 and 6 by reinforcing the food and water systems, SDG 7 by promoting renewable energy, SDG 11 through sustainable urban planning, and SDGs 14 and 15 by protecting ecosystems and biodiversity. This serves as a reminder and urges people to be alert to the necessity of mitigating climate change and its consequences and to take action to produce synergistic results that maximise positive impacts on sustainable development in order to promote resilient communities that support health, well-being, and sustainability.

In summary, each component of the environment and ecosystems is as critical as the key determinants of improved population health. Policymakers, academics, healthcare professionals, and individuals should recognise the importance of healthy environments and encourage multi-disciplinary collaboration, as the relationship between the environmental and ecological determinants of health and the SDGs is complex and complementary. By integrating environmental and ecological considerations into policies and promoting sustainable practices, the overall health and well-being of individuals and communities can be improved. Furthermore, the continued provision of vital ecosystem services can be supported and the attainment of SDGs can be facilitated, creating a healthier and more sustainable future for all.

## Impacts From Critical Health Issues and Events

The old saying "prevention is better than cure" means preventing or stopping unwanted problems from happening, rather than solving or correcting them after they have occurred. Making efforts to prevent illnesses can help people maintain good physical health, which is just one of the ways to keep everyone healthy. Even though there is much health-related information and regular disease-preventing practices that are continuously being disseminated to educate people, there is still the possibility of health-related issues arising and posing a threat to health. In the context of globalisation, in which the world is closely interconnected, health issues may arise on a global scale, and such a critical situation can have even more serious impacts and devastating consequences because the occurrence of critical health issues is not confined to geographical boundaries. Simply, infectious diseases can spread from a small village to a prosperous city or even an entire continent; and non-communicable diseases are causing three-fourths of global deaths, particularly in low- and middle-income countries (WHO, 2023b).

Despite the partial success achieved in the healthcare sector over the last century, which has increased life expectancy, reduced mortality from certain diseases, and developed health science and technology innovations, the world still confronts serious health-related threats. In fact, critical health issues, especially outbreaks of infectious diseases, have occurred throughout recorded history, from the plague, cholera, Spanish Flu, human immunodeficiency virus (HIV), Ebola, and the COVID-19 pandemic (Sampath et al., 2021). WHO (2020) has updated and shortlisted several health challenges, such as ensuring worldwide health security, strengthening universal health systems for all, tackling health inequities, responding to mental health problems, and so forth. The previous unfulfilment has exposed the deficiencies in the health systems and the potential for outbreaks of health issues.

There is a general rule that when certain things happen, certain consequences follow. Critical health issues have far-reaching impacts on both the global economy and ecosystems (Ibn-Mohammed et al., 2021; McKibbin & Fernando, 2020). The outbreak of diseases can disrupt trade, productivity, and supply chains, leading to economic downturns and social upheaval, as the world has witnessed and experienced during the recent pandemic. Simultaneously, these health issues can also have profound effects on the environment and ecosystems, altering biodiversity and ecological balance. The following section explores the impacts of critical health issues on the global economy and ecosystems, as exemplified by recent events such as the COVID-19 pandemic, highlighting the need for preparedness and possible insights for response.

## Impacts on the Global Economy

### *Economic Disruptions*

Critical health issues have not only triggered health crises but also had a significant impact on the global economy, leading to global recession and economic contraction, affecting various sectors and populations around the world. The relationship between critical health issues and economic disruptions is intricate. The outbreak of COVID-19 has indeed caused substantial global economic disruption and losses on an unprecedented scale.

Following the WHO's declaration of COVID-19 as a public health emergency of international concern, strict social isolation and lockdown measures were implemented in many countries, and people's lifestyles and behaviours were altered. Changes in consumption behaviour were reflected in purchasing demands and patterns, as people preferred to buy more food and sanitary products due to panic and fear of disease infection or difficulty in accessing goods and services in a state of social distancing and isolation. This has also led to concerns about necessities and affordability, and people might decide to reduce spending. As a result, industries such as tourism, transportation, and hospitality were particularly vulnerable at that time, experiencing reduced demand, closures of businesses, and massive layoffs. The lower consumption led to decreased business sales, further reducing labour demand and in turn reducing household consumption.

The economic repercussions of health crises like the COVID-19 pandemic go beyond healthcare costs. They encompass failures in healthcare systems, missed economic market opportunities, and relevant socioeconomic consequences, such as unemployment, poverty, and social unwellness. As the impact of critical health issues on the global economy has led to significant disruptions in economic activities, the collateral effects of critical health issues, including the global economic downturns and social isolation measures, disproportionately impact vulnerable groups and exacerbate existing inequalities (Chen et al., 2022; Shadmi et al., 2020).

### *Trade and Supply Chain Disruptions*

Critical health issues can also lead to significant disruptions in trade and supply chains. The COVID-19 pandemic serves as a recent example of how critical health issues can expose vulnerabilities in trade and supply chains, leading to disruptions in the flow of goods and services locally and globally, and necessitating strategic responses to mitigate the economic and operational impacts of such disruptions.

Drugs, vaccines, personal protective equipment (PPE), single-use equipment, laboratory and test-related supplies, and other medical devices and consumables are essential commodities and supplies that support treatment, disease prevention, infection control, and responsive activities. The COVID-19 pandemic has excessively strained the global health systems, with a surge in demand for medical supplies. However, production of products was suspended, and market access was restricted, resulting in shortages of critical medical supplies and medicines (Okafor et al., 2021). The outbreak of COVID-19 has also highlighted vulnerabilities in supply chains, with disruptions occurring due to factors such as border closures, national and regional lockdowns, transportation restrictions, and international trade limitations adopted in response to the health crisis. These disruptions had impeded the flow of goods, services, and raw materials. Therefore, global trade was disrupted by delays in production and delivery, leading to massive economic losses (Safwen & Németh, 2021).

Disruptions in global trade and supply chains have many consequences. During the COVID-19 pandemic, trade and supply chain disruptions affected not only the immediate production and delivery of goods and services, influencing the organisational performance, but also the risk, profitability, and sources of financing for firms in the supply chain (Gibilaro & Mattarocci, 2019). As deficiencies in current supply chain operations have been exposed, this emphasises the need for companies to allocate resources wisely in order to fulfil orders during disruptions based on priorities and trade-offs (Zhu et al., 2020).

### *Impacts on the Ecosystems*

Health is closely linked to ecosystems, and biodiversity should be protected. It is because ecosystems are vulnerable to disruption, leading to the loss of biodiversity and undermining of essential ecosystem services (such as clean air and water, pollination, and climate regulation). Critical health issues can lead to the loss of biodiversity through a variety of mechanisms that can have profound effects on ecosystems and disturb the delicate balance of the natural environment.

Disruptions in ecosystems can have far-reaching impacts on both health and the environment. During the COVID-19 pandemic, the loss of biodiversity was further exacerbated by anthropogenic factors, for example, the rollback of air quality and biodiversity regulations, despite concerns about the links between pollution, wildlife, and habitat destruction (Nyiwul, 2023). The relationship between the loss of biodiversity, high levels of air pollutants, declining air quality, and the spread and mortality of COVID-19 favoured the emergence of the virus, allowing the pandemic to occur (Fernández et al., 2021). Zoonoses are the root cause of disease transmission, and their emergence and spread will increase the risk of future health crises if wildlife is not protected and conserved.

While the COVID-19 pandemic has had negative impacts on various aspects of society, including biodiversity, there have been some positive effects on natural resources. The reduction in pollutants and noise pollution during lockdowns had positive effects on aquatic ecosystems, water quality, wildlife behaviour, and ecosystem restoration (Muche et al., 2022). The pandemic has also shed light on the environmental and biodiversity crisis, providing an opportunity to redefine humanity's relationship with nature (Cooke et al., 2021). More attention, engagement, and proactive measures are therefore needed to mitigate the impacts. In times of crisis, such as the current global emergency of declining biodiversity and climate change, reconnecting with nature and understanding the contribution of the environment and ecosystems to health and well-being becomes crucial (Benessaiah & Chan, 2023). Addressing the root causes and promoting sustainable practices can help prevent further loss of biodiversity and build a more resilient environment for the future.

In general, critical health issues would impact the global economy and ecosystems. The COVID-19 pandemic has highlighted the significance of responding to global health threats and their impacts on all levels of the society, the global economy and ecosystems, demonstrating that critical health issues can have a range of impacts and challenges to the world. In order to address these impacts, it is important to prioritise preparedness, strengthen healthcare systems, adopt sustainable approaches, and promote international cooperation. By integrating sustainable development and health approaches, everyone can be better able to mitigate the impacts of critical health issues on the global economy and ecosystems and promote a more resilient and sustainable future. It is important to note that the impacts discussed in this section may vary depending on the specific health issue and its severity. Further research and analysis are needed to fully understand the complex interactions between health, the economy, and ecosystems in the context of critical health issues.

## One Health: Integrating Population, Environmental and Ecological Health for a Sustainable Future

When discussing solutions or remedies to deal with different healthcare-related issues, many researchers and professionals recommend multidisciplinary collaboration to build partnerships and enhance coordination. In the wake of the COVID-19 pandemic, an unprecedented collision of global health systems has exposed and revealed current deficiencies or structural weaknesses, necessitating the need to address these underlying problems and the likelihood of similar severe health crises. In order to foster and contribute to building a sustainable and healthy world for the population, the "One Health" approach is then accentuated and promoted, which emphasises the need to holistically tackle health-related problems. One Health is a multidisciplinary conceptual approach that advocates integrative health practices, interconnecting human, environmental (including animals and plants), and ecological health.

### *Understanding One Health*

People can benefit from utilising animals and natural resources in their daily lives as food and pets, while human activities may affect the natural environment and alter the habitats. The interactions between humans, animals, and the environment are dynamic and complex. Humans are living with domestic and wild animals, so health is closely linked to the shared environment. The concept of the "One Health" approach has emerged. As defined by the WHO (2023d), One Health is an approach that mobilises multi-sectoral, inter-disciplinary parties and integrates human, animal, and ecological health to obtain an optimal status and sustainability (Centers for Disease Control and Prevention [CDC], 2023).

In fact, the One Health approach is not an innovative concept. Similarities between human and animal disease processes were observed and identified as early as the nineteenth century, as the relevant concept had roots in early epidemiological studies that recognised the role of animals in the transmission of human diseases, when Dr Calvin Schwab revived a prototypical idea and first introduced the term "One Medicine" to link human and veterinary medicine. Over time, it has evolved to encompass a broader range of environmental and ecological considerations, and One Medicine has been transformed into One Health (CDC, 2022). Although the name has changed, the concepts can still be discussed and inspired for further modification, and some of the new concepts can be updated and inherited from the old ones, which contributes to a better knowledge and understanding of health.

Bresalier et al. (2021) described One Health as the inheritor to One Medicine, which aims to build a healthy and sustainable world by promoting and addressing health issues at the human–animal–environment interface. As an interdisciplinary approach, this ideational concept requires collaboration across various disciplines, such as medicine, veterinary science, ecology, public health, and environmental science, as well as integrative efforts to work in the community, from regional, national, and even global scales to promote a holistic understanding of health challenges and facilitates the development of effective solutions.

### *Importance of One Health*

One Health targets and supports global health, and there are a number of issues or challenges that need to be eliminated with respect to One Health, such as zoonotic diseases, anti-microbial resistance, food safety and security, climate change adaptation, and so on. Therefore, it is important to implement such an approach for health promotion and sustainable development.

Firstly, the One Health approach helps to improve zoonotic disease prevention and control. Owing to the close relationship between humans and animals, many emerging infectious diseases, namely COVID-19, Mpox (formerly known as monkeypox), SARS, Ebola, and avian influenza, are zoonotic in nature, leading to a variety of health and socioeconomic consequences. Horefti (2023) summarises some cases, including rabies, Hendra virus, MERS, and Zika virus infections, where the One Health approach has been used to mitigate zoonosis-based problems. Health professionals follow the

One Health approach to help control and minimise the spread of zoonotic diseases through surveillance, early detection, and rapid response. Professionals from different disciplines collaborate and share expertise, and outline strategic plans for zoonotic disease management. Besides, based on current knowledge of zoonotic diseases, pathological investigations and continuous monitoring are conducted, and relevant disease prevention information or One Health-associated measures are further implemented and disseminated to the public. As a result, the capacity of the One Health approach to assist in the prevention of zoonotic diseases has been recognised.

Secondly, the One Health approach promotes responsible antimicrobial use, reduces the spread of resistance, and preserves the effectiveness of these vital drugs. Antibiotics are life-saving medicines, which can treat bacterial infections. However, the misuse and overuse of antibiotics in human and animal healthcare are leading to the development of antimicrobial resistance, for example, resistance to colistin, third-generation cephalosporins and fluoroquinolones, which is also a growing global health concern (Velazquez-Meza et al., 2022). The consequences of antimicrobial resistance are followed by ineffective antimicrobial therapy, increased risk and severity of infections, and contamination of the environment, food, and trade chains (Collignon & McEwen, 2019; Rousham et al., 2018). Therefore, adopting One Health strategies to combat antimicrobial resistance is essential to tackling health issues. Cella et al. (2023) explained that the core concept of One Health is to establish surveillance systems, implement policy decisions, perform relevant research, and disseminate interventional measures so as to integrate the direction of various fields and specialities and develop practical methods to respond to the problem.

Lastly, the One Health approach is essential to sustainable development. It is assumed that the 17 SDGs and related targets will be achieved by 2030, but the world has already reached the halfway mark and there is only limited time left to meet the deadline ("Halfway to 2030", 2023). As discussed earlier, the SDGs are closely linked to health and are multifaceted and multidisciplinary, and so the One Health approach can provide a unifying framework for achieving these goals. Queenan et al. (2017) argued that the One Health approach could synergise sustainable development. They suggested that an understanding of the relationship between health and the environment could raise public awareness of political-social-economic-environmental (ecological)-health impacts and encourage amelioration or mitigation of these issues, ranging from thoughtful approaches to policies and practical interventions developed for a sustainable and healthy future. Furthermore, the One Health High-Level Expert Panel (OHHLEP) et al. (2022) have mentioned that the application of the One Health principles is consistent with the concept of sustainable development and emphasised the potential of this approach to address a wide range of health issues.

By recognising the importance of the One Health approach, it provides a problem-solving framework with a clear potential for developing human–animal–environmental health. This is because the One Health approach is integrative and helps to bridge the gaps between science and policy, knowledge and implementation, expertise and practice, vision, and reality.

### *Challenges and Opportunities*

Embracing the One Health approach contributes to sustainable development, strengthens resilience, and creates a healthier future for current and future generations. As a result, the One Health approach is receiving attention and discussion after the COVID-19 pandemic, but many challenges remain due to the nature of its conceptual scope.

To begin with, a limited interdisciplinary collaboration is one of the major challenges for adopting the One Health approach. Encouraging collaboration across different disciplines and sectors can be difficult due to differences in priorities, perspectives, and institutional structures. In addition, coordinating concepts, principles, policies, regulations, and governance structures across sectors can be complex. Yopa et al. (2023) elaborated on some reasons that impede the difficulties of interdisciplinary collaboration, which are particularly serious in developing countries. They identified political instability, regional tensions and conflicts, mistrust among political elites, and limited resources and capacity as obstacles to the implementation of One Health interdisciplinary collaboration.

The second challenge is the linkage between One Health and other health-related concepts or systems. The targeted applications of the One Health approach cover food safety, control of zoonotic diseases, laboratory services, neglected tropical diseases, environmental health, and antimicrobial resistance. While the One Health approach involves multiple disciplines, its application only partially addresses threats to human, animal, and environmental health as Destoumieux-Garzón et al. (2018) highlighted that wildlife and other ecological, social, legal, and economic components were omitted in One Health. Dye (2022) further argued that One Health replicated the concepts of "Health in All Policies" and "whole of society" approaches and not completely linked to the SDGs. While different health approaches have similar or even the same core values, if the goals and targets are not aligned, people do not know whether and how to take precise actions.

In addition, recognising and measuring the impacts of One Health is another challenge. Sinclair (2019) revealed that there was a lack of standardisation in assessing the risks of One Health issues and evaluating the impacts of One Health implementation. This is because the One Health approach only provides, in writing, the directional objectives that need to be achieved. For instance, the global One Health index (GOHI) has been proposed as a parameter for assessing One Health performance, but it is only at the development stage and still needs to be validated and further consolidated before it can be applied in the real world (Zhang et al., 2022). It is difficult to measure the impacts of One Health implementation without developing assessment indicators or guidelines on evaluation methods.

It is important to enhance the One Health approach for promoting health and sustainable development. A successful implementation of One Health requires global commitment, collaborative efforts, policy support, sharing knowledge, resources, and best practices among nations, all of which can enhance preparedness, response capacity, and sustainable recovery efforts to further advance the One Health approach and unlock its full potential to address the complex critical health issues of our time. If everyone strives to see and confront challenges as opportunities to turn problems into progress, this will substantially increase the chance of success.

## Achieving Sustainable Health and Development Through One Health

### *Addressing Climate Change*

Climate change poses significant risks which affect all aspects of society, including food security, water availability, and disease patterns. Addressing climate change can mitigate environmental risks and provide opportunities to promote health and sustainable development. Effective responses to climate change require a comprehensive approach. The One Health approach incorporates climate change considerations, recognising the complex interactions between health and the environment. Mitigating the effects of climate change and adapting to them are essential to safeguarding the health of humans, animals, and the environment, and integrating climate change adaptation into health practices can increase adaptive capacity and resilience, as highlighted by the concept of One Health (Hess et al., 2012).

Adaptation to climate change is crucial, especially in developing countries where vulnerability is high. Environmental protection measures provide the basic direction for addressing environmental problems and reducing the damaging effects on the climate. Construction can be a slow and laborious task of years, while destruction can be a thoughtless act in just a single moment. No one can guarantee the time and extent of ecosystem restoration required, and the community have to counteract climate change and preserve ecosystems in the long term. Mitigation and adaptation strategies are not only addressing climate change but also providing positive co-benefits for the health of the population (Bikomeye et al., 2021). For example, the need for more advanced strategies for the impacts of climate change on disasters and emergency medicine is mentioned, including the implementation of emergency management, enhancement of emergency services, equipment and resources, and increased awareness of the risks associated with climate change, in order to mitigate the health risks associated with extreme weather event (Ghazali et al., 2018). Professionals in the health industry also play a crucial role in addressing climate change and promoting sustainable development (Nicholas & Breakey, 2017). Therefore, strategies for mitigating and adapting to the health impacts of climate change are essential for promoting population health and sustainable development.

### *Conserving Biodiversity*

Biodiversity encompasses all living organisms and their interactions, including plants, animals, and microorganisms, as well as their ecosystems. By recognising the value of intact ecosystems, One Health supports conservation efforts and environmentally sustainable practices based on human well-being and ecosystem services. Conserving biodiversity increases resilience, reduces disease risk, and supports sustainable development.

Maintaining intact ecosystems is crucial for halting the ongoing biodiversity crisis. A healthy and sustainable ecosystem contributes to clean air and water, nutrient cycling, and climate regulation which are essential to the promotion of good health and well-being. Pillay et al. (2022) have suggested that protecting more structurally intact forests, which act as natural filters for improving air quality and reducing respiratory diseases, reduces the risk of extinction of vertebrates in the humid tropics, emphasising the need to reduce deforestation to conserve global biodiversity. In addition, successful management of urban green spaces is included because it prioritises biological complexity and enhances human well-being while conserving biodiversity. Conservation planning and strategies focusing on biodiversity conservation in a changing climate can safeguard essential ecosystem services (Buotte et al., 2019).

Conservation of biodiversity is seen as fundamentally vital, highlighting its key role in ecosystem resilience and sustainability. It also contributes to cultural and recreational values by integrating biodiversity conservation with ecotourism management, providing opportunities for recreation as well as spiritual and cultural experiences (Zoysa, 2022). Access to nature and biodiversity-rich areas helps achieving improved mental health, reduced stress, increased physical activity, and enhanced public awareness on biodiversity conservation. With proper management and strategies, it ensures the conservation of unique landscapes and functionality, biodiversity hotspots, and cultural heritage, enhancing the quality of life for individuals and communities (Bosch et al., 2023).

### *Integrating Health and Medicine Approach*

Instead of continuously proposing more new approaches or concepts, which are changing day by day and may not be aligned with reality when they are put into practice, it is better to utilise and integrate the existing approaches and concepts, followed by further development of their strengths. Chinese medicine (CM), for example, is rooted in the traditional Chinese culture and practice. It offers a unique perspective and approach to healthcare that is consistent with the principles of sustainability, holistic care, and interconnectedness, utilising natural and traditional resources for a contemporary healthcare approach. The benefits of using CM in therapies have been reported widely, and there are also growing studies investigating the public perception and attitude towards the use of CM in healthcare (Ng et al., 2022).

By combining CM with modern treatments in an integrative medicine approach, the utilisation of CM ideas can be employed to engage people in healthcare and promote health awareness, contributing to the sustainability of healthcare practices (Shahrajabian et al., 2019a). The integration of CM with Western medicine can lead to improved health and a more comprehensive healthcare system. It is possible to enhance the accessibility, affordability, and effectiveness of healthcare services and promote preventive healthcare and overall health practices, such as acupuncture, herbal medicine, and dietary therapy (Pan & Zhou, 2013). Governments can establish policies and frameworks that encourage collaboration between Chinese medicine practitioners and conventional healthcare providers. For example, China is a pioneer in implementing pilot projects that integrate CM into primary healthcare systems, ensuring that patients can benefit from both traditional and modern approaches.

Herbal medicines derived from plants are widely used in CM and can play an important role in sustainable agriculture and food systems through the promotion of organic farming practices, biodiversity conservation, and the appropriate use of herbal products (Shahrajabian et al., 2019b). Promoting sustainable agricultural practices can reduce environmental impacts, prioritise animal welfare and enhance food security. At the same time, it ensures the availability of high-quality herbs while protecting the ecosystem. These practices include organic farming, agroecology, and the responsible use of natural resources, supporting the cultivation of medicinal plants without degrading and damaging the environment. For instance, the use of traditional farming techniques and wild herb conservation are promoted in China's Good Agricultural Practice (GAP) certification standards for CM.

In short, integrating CM into efforts to achieve the SDGs and promote One Health, the community can capitalise on the strengths of CM in preventive care, personalised treatment, and health promotion with modern healthcare practices, which would lead to sustainable health by providing a holistic approach, promoting organic and herbal therapies, raising individual healthcare awareness, and utilising technological advancement to improve health management and population health in the world.

## Conclusion

In addition to personal health and wellness, population health is also important, with due consideration of environmental and ecological factors. Throughout the community development process, neither individuals nor parties are involved in health issues as detached observers or bystanders. Community development does not violate the principles of environmental protection and preservation. The One Health approach can bring enormous socio-economic benefits. One Health contributes to preventing disease, ensuring access to food, water, sanitation, and energy, protecting the environment and ecosystem, promoting sustainable practices and improving social well-being. By regaining the harmony between humans, resources, and environments, everyone should work collaboratively in attaining a healthy and sustainable environment for the current and future generations.

## References


Agache, I., Sampath, V., Aguilera, J., Akdis, C. A., Akdis, M., Barry, M., Bouagnon, A., Chinthrajah, S., Collins, W., Dulitzki, C., Erny, B., Gomez, J., Goshua, A., Jutel, M., Kizer, K. W., Kline, O., LaBeaud, A. D., Pali-Schöll, I., Perrett, K. P., . . . & Nadeau, K. C. (2022). Climate change and global health: A call to more research and more action. *Allergy*, *77*(5), 1389–1407. https://doi.org/10.1111/all.15229

Arora, N. K., & Mishra, I. (2022). Sustainable development goal 6: Global Water Security. *Environmental Sustainability*, *5*, 271–275. https://doi.org/10.1007/s42398-022-00246-5

Benessaiah, K., & Chan, K. M. (2023). Why reconnect to nature in times of crisis? Ecosystem contributions to the resilience and well-being of people going back to the land in Greece. *People and Nature*, *5*(6), 2026–2047. https://doi.org/10.1002/pan3.10546

Bikomeye, J. C., Rublee, C. S., & Beyer, K. M. M. (2021). Positive externalities of climate change mitigation and adaptation for human health: A review and conceptual framework for public health research. *International Journal of Environmental Research and Public Health*, *18*(5), 2481. https://doi.org/10.3390/ijerph18052481

Bosch, N. E., Espino, F. E., Tuya, F., Haroun, R., Bramanti, L., & Otero-Ferrer, F. (2023). Black coral forests enhance taxonomic and functional distinctiveness of mesophotic fishes in an oceanic island: Implications for biodiversity conservation. *Scientific Reports*, *13*, 4963. https://doi.org/10.1038/s41598-023-32138-x

Bresalier, M., Cassidy, A., & Woods, A. (2021). One health in history. In J. Zinsstag, E. Schelling, L. Crump, M. Whittaker, M. Tanner, & C. Stephen (Eds.), *One health: The theory and practice of integrated health approaches* (2nd ed., pp. 1–14). CAB International. http://doi.org/10.1079/9781789242577.0001

Buotte, P. C., Law, B. E., Ripple, W. J., & Berner, L. T. (2019). Carbon sequestration and biodiversity co-benefits of preserving forests in the western United States. *Ecological Applications*, *30*(2), e02039. https://doi.org/10.1002/eap.2039

Cella, E., Giovanetti, M., Benedetti, F., Scarpa, F., Johnston, C., Borsetti, A., Ceccarelli, G., Azarian, T., Zella, D., & Ciccozzi, M. (2023). Joining forces against antibiotic resistance: The one health solution. *Pathogens*, *12*(9), 1074. https://doi.org/10.3390/pathogens12091074

Centers for Disease Control and Prevention. (2022, June 6). *One health basics history*. www.cdc.gov/onehealth/basics/history/index.html

Centers for Disease Control and Prevention. (2023, September 28). *One health basics*. www.cdc.gov/onehealth/basics/index.html

Centers for Medicare and Medicaid Services. (2023, December). *Population health measures*. https://mmshub.cms.gov/sites/default/files/Population-Health-Measures.pdf

Central Intelligence Agency. (n.d.). *The World Factbook field listing – Food insecurity*. www.cia.gov/the-world-factbook/field/food-insecurity/

Chen, J., Chou, S. Y., Yu, T. H., Rizqi, Z. U., & Hang, D. T. (2022). System dynamics analysis on the effectiveness of vaccination and social mobilization policies for COVID-19 in the United States. *PLoS ONE*, *17*(8), e0268443. https://doi.org/10.1371/journal.pone.0268443

Chiu, W. K. (2021). Pedagogy of emerging technologies in chemical education during the era of digitalization and artificial intelligence: A systematic review. *Education Sciences*, *11*(11), 709. https://doi.org/10.3390/educsci11110709

Chiu, W. K., & Fong, B. Y. F. (2022). Chemical pollution and healthy ageing: The prominent need for a cleaner environment. In V. T. S. Law & B. Y. F. Fong (Eds.), *Ageing with dignity in Hong Kong and Asia*(pp. 277–287). Springer. https://doi.org/10.1007/978-981-19-3061-4_19

Climate Science Investigations. (2023, April 3). *Causes of climate change*. www.ces.fau.edu/nasa/module-4/causes-2.php

Collignon, P. J., & McEwen, S. A. (2019). One health – Its importance in helping to better control antimicrobial resistance. *Tropical Medicine and Infectious Disease, 4*(1), 22. https://doi.org/10.3390/tropicalmed4010022

Cooke, S. J., Soroye, R., Brooks, J. L., Clarke, J., Jeanson, A. L., Berberi, A., Piczak, M. L., Reid, C. H., Desforges, J. E., Guay, J. D., Drake, A. K., Jardine, A. M., Ethier, J. P., Keefe, H. E., Medd, A. M., Edwards, B. P. M., Reeve, C., Perkovic, A., Frempong-Manso, A., . . . & Bennett, J. R. (2021). Ten considerations for conservation policy makers for the post-COVID-19 transition. *Environmental Reviews, 29*(2), 111–118. https://doi.org/10.1139/er-2021-0014

Department of Economic and Social Affairs, The United Nations. (n.d.). *Goals 6 ensure availability and sustainable management of water and sanitation for all.* https://sdgs.un.org/goals/goal6

Destoumieux-Garzón, D., Mavingui, P., Boetsch, G., Boissier, J., Darriet, F., Duboz, P., Fritsch, C., Giraudoux, P., Le Roux, F., Morand, S., Paillard, C., Pontier, D., Sueur, C., & Voituron, Y. (2018). The one health concept: 10 years old and a long road ahead. *Frontiers in Veterinary Science, 5*, 14. https://doi.org/10.3389/fvets.2018.00014

Dhunna, S., & Tarasuk, V. (2021). Black–white racial disparities in household food insecurity from 2005 to 2014, Canada. *Canadian Journal of Public Health, 112*, 888–902. https://doi.org/10.17269/s41997-021-00539-y

Driga, A. M., & Drigas, A. S. (2019). Climate change 101: How everyday activities contribute to the ever-growing issue. *International Journal of Recent Contributions from Engineering, Science & IT (iJES), 7*(1), 22–31. https://doi.org/10.3991/ijes.v7i1.10031

Dye, C. (2022). One health as a catalyst for sustainable development. *Nature Microbiology, 7*, 467–468. https://doi.org/10.1038/s41564-022-01076-1

Ebi, K. L., Vanos, J., Baldwin, J. W., Bell, J. E., Hondula, D. M., Errett, N. A., Hayes, K., Reid, C. E., Saha, S., Spector, J., & Berry, P. (2021). Extreme weather and climate change: Population health and health system implications. *Annual Review of Public Health, 42*, 293–315. https://doi.org/10.1146/annurev-publhealth-012420-105026

Economist Impact. (n.d.). *Global food security index 2022.* https://impact.economist.com/sustainability/project/food-security-index/

Fernández, D., Giné-Vázquez, I., Liu, I., Yucel, R., Nai Ruscone, M., Morena, M., García, V. G., Haro, J. M., Pan, W., & Tyrovolas, S. (2021). Are environmental pollution and biodiversity levels associated to the spread and mortality of COVID-19? A four-month global analysis. *Environmental Pollution, 271*, 116326. https://doi.org/10.1016/j.envpol.2020.116326

Fong, B. Y. F., & Chiu, W. K. (2023). A systems approach to achieving health for all in the community. In B. Y. F. Fong & W. C. W. Wong (Eds.), *Gaps and actions in health improvement from Hong Kong and Beyond* (pp. 41–54). Springer. https://doi.org/10.1007/978-981-99-4491-0_4

Food and Agriculture Organization of the United Nations. (n.d.). *Hunger and food insecurity*. www.fao.org/hunger/en/

Food insecurity: A public health issue. (2016). *Public Health Reports, 131*(5), 655–657. https://doi.org/10.1177/0033354916664154

Fuso Nerini, F., Sovacool, B., Hughes, N., Cozzi, L., Cosgrave, E., Howells, M., Tavoni, M., Tomei, J., Zerriffi, H., & Milligan, B. (2019). Connecting climate action with other Sustainable Development Goals. *Nature Sustainability, 2*(8), 674–680. https://doi.org/10.1038/s41893-019-0334-y

Fuso Nerini, F., Tomei, J., To, L. S., Bisaga, I., Parikh, P., Black, M., Borrion, A., Spataru, C., Broto, V. C., Anandarajah, G., Milligan, B., & Mulugetta, Y. (2018). Mapping synergies and trade-offs between energy and the Sustainable Development Goals. *Nature Energy*, *3*, 10–15. https://doi.org/10.1038/s41560-017-0036-5

Ghazali, D. A., Guericolas, M., Thys, F., Sarasin, F., González, P. A., & Casalino, E. (2018). Climate change impacts on disaster and emergency medicine focusing on mitigation disruptive effects: An international perspective. *International Journal of Environmental Research and Public Health*, *15*(7), 1379. https://doi.org/10.3390/ijerph15071379

Gibilaro, L., & Mattarocci, G. (2019). The impact of corporate distress along the supply chain: Evidences from United States. *Supply Chain Management*, *24*(4), 498–508. https://doi.org/10.1108/SCM-08-2018-0275

The Global Goals. (n.d.). *Goal 3: Good health and well-being*. www.globalgoals.org/goals/3-good-health-and-well-being/

Halfway to 2030, world 'nowhere near' reaching Global Goals, UN warns. (2023, July 17). *UN News*. https://news.un.org/en/story/2023/07/1138777

Hess, J. J., McDowell, J. Z., & Luber, G. (2012). Integrating climate change adaptation into public health practice: Using adaptive management to increase adaptive capacity and build resilience. *Environmental Health Perspectives*, *120*(2), 171–179. https://doi.org/10.1289/ehp.1103515

Horefti, E. (2023). The importance of the one health concept in combating zoonoses. *Pathogens*, *12*(8), 977. https://doi.org/10.3390/pathogens12080977

Howard, G. (2021). The future of water and sanitation: Global challenges and the need for greater ambition. *AQUA – Water Infrastructure, Ecosystems and Society*, *70*(4), 438–448. https://doi.org/10.2166/aqua.2021.127

Ibn-Mohammed, T., Mustapha, K. B., Godsell, J., Adamu, Z., Babatunde, K. A., Akintade, D. D., Acquaye, A., Fujii, H., Ndiaye, M. M., Yamoah, F. A., & Koh, S. C. L. (2021). A critical analysis of the impacts of COVID-19 on the global economy and ecosystems and opportunities for circular economy strategies. *Resources, Conservation and Recycling*, *164*, 105169. https://doi.org/10.1016/j.resconrec.2020.105169

The International Energy Agency. (2023). *Access to electricity – SDG7: Data and projections*. www.iea.org/reports/sdg7-data-and-projections/access-to-electricity

Kindig, D., & Stoddart, G. (2003). What is population health?. *American Journal of Public Health*, *93*(3), 380–383. https://doi.org/10.2105/ajph.93.3.380

Lam, H. M., Remais, J., Fung, M. C., Xu, L., & Sun, S. S. M. (2013). Food supply and food safety issues in China. *The Lancet*, *381*(9882), 2044–2053. https://doi.org/10.1016/S0140-6736(13)60776-X

McKibbin, W. J., & Fernando, R. (2020). Global macroeconomic scenarios of the COVID-19 pandemic. *CAMA Working Paper No. 62/2020*. http://doi.org/10.2139/ssrn.3635103

Muche, M., Yemata, G., Molla, E., Muasya, A. M., & Tsegay, B. A. (2022). COVID-19 lockdown and natural resources: A global assessment on the challenges, opportunities, and the way forward. *Bulletin of the National Research Centre*, *46*, 20. https://doi.org/10.1186/s42269-022-00706-2

Ng, T. K., Lo, M. F., & Fong, B. Y. (2022). Knowledge, attitude, utilisation and satisfaction of traditional Chinese medicine in Hong Kong. *International Journal of Pharmaceutical and Healthcare Marketing*, *16*(1), 123–137. https://doi.org/10.1108/IJPHM-08-2020-0068

Nicholas, P. K., & Breakey, S. (2017). Climate change, climate justice, and environmental health: Implications for the nursing profession. *Journal of Nursing Scholarship*, *49*(6), 606–616. https://doi.org/10.1111/jnu.12326

Nyiwul, L. M. (2023). COVID-19 and the environmental regulatory response: Compendium of regulatory, ad hoc changes and implications. *Environmental Protection Research*, *3*(1), 26–37. https://doi.org/10.37256/epr.3120232046

Okafor, U. G., Olaleye, M. A., Asobara, H. C., & Umeodinka, E. F. (2021). Global impact of COVID-19 pandemic on public health supply chains. In E. Guerrero (Ed.), *Science-based approaches to respond to COVID and other public health threats* (pp. 87–102). IntechOpen. http://doi.org/10.5772/intechopen.97454

One Health High-Level Expert Panel (OHHLEP), Adisasmito, W. B., Almuhairi, S., Behravesh, C. B., Bilivogui, P., Bukachi, S. A., Casas, N., Cediel Becerra, N., Charron, D. F., Chaudhary, A., Ciacci Zanella, J. R., Cunningham, A. A., Dar, O., Debnath, N., Dungu, B., Farag, E., Gao, G. F., Hayman, D. T. S., Khaitsa, M., . . . & Zhou, L. (2022). One health: A new definition for a sustainable and healthy future. *PLoS Pathogens*, *18*(6), e1010537. https://doi.org/10.1371/journal.ppat.1010537

Pan, W., & Zhou, H. (2013). Integrative medicine: A paradigm shift in clinical practice. *International Journal of Integrative Medicine*, *1*. https://doi.org/10.5772/56817

Pérez-Escamilla, R. (2017). Food security and the 2015–2030 sustainable development goals: From human to planetary health: Perspectives and opinions. *Current Developments in Nutrition*, *1*(7), e000513. https://doi.org/10.3945/cdn.117.000513

Pillay, R., Watson, J. E. M., Hansen, A. J., Jantz, P. A., Aragon-Osejo, J., Armenteras, D., Atkinson, S. C., Burns, P., Ervin, J., Goetz, S. J., González-del-Pliego, P., Robinson, N. P., Supples, C., Virnig, A. L. S., Williams, B. A., & Venter, O. (2022). Humid tropical vertebrates are at lower risk of extinction and population decline in forests with higher structural integrity. *Nature Ecology and Evolution*, *6*(12), 1840–1849. https://doi.org/10.1038/s41559-022-01915-8

Porcaro, J., Mehta, S., Shupler, M., Kissel, S., Pfeiffer, M., Dora, C. F. C., & Adair-Rohani, H. (2017, June 13). *Modern energy access and health*. World Health Organization. https://doi.org/10.1596/26648

Pourmotabbed, A., Moradi, S., Babaei, A., Ghavami, A., Mohammadi, H., Jalili, C., Symonds, M. E., & Miraghajani, M. (2020). Food insecurity and mental health: A systematic review and meta-analysis. *Public Health Nutrition*, *23*(10), 1778–1790. https://doi.org/10.1017/s136898001900435x

Queenan, K., Garnier, J., Nielsen, L. R., Buttigieg, S., de Meneghi, D., Holmberg, M., Zinsstag, J., Rüegg, S., Häsler, B., & Kock, R. (2017). Roadmap to a one health agenda 2030. *CABI Reviews*, *12*(14). http://doi.org/10.1079/PAVSNNR201712014

Rousham, E. K., Unicomb, L., & Islam, M. A. (2018). Human, animal and environmental contributors to antibiotic resistance in low-resource settings: Integrating behavioural, epidemiological and one health approaches. *Proceedings of the Royal Society B: Biological Sciences*, *285*(1867), 20180332. https://doi.org/10.1098/rspb.2018.0332

Safwen, B. N., & Németh, P. (2021). Physical internet: A solution for the Supply Chain disruptions during the COVID-19 pandemic. *Acta Technica Jaurinensis*, *14*(4), 577–598. https://doi.org/10.14513/actatechjaur.00579

Sampath, S., Khedr, A., Qamar, S., Tekin, A., Singh, R., Green, R., & Kashyap, R. (2021). Pandemics throughout the history. *Cureus*, *13*(9), e18136. https://doi.org/10.7759/cureus.18136

Shadmi, E., Chen, Y., Dourado, I., Faran-Perach, I., Furler, J., Hangoma, P., Hanvoravongchai, P., Obando, C., Petrosyan, V., Rao, K. D., Ruano, A. L., Shi, L., de Souza, L. E., Spitzer-Shohat, S., Sturgiss, E., Suphanchaimat, R., Uribe, M. V., & Willems, S. (2020). Health equity and COVID-19: Global perspectives. *International Journal for Equity in Health*, *19*(1), 104. https://doi.org/10.1186/s12939-020-01218-z

Shahrajabian, M. H., Sun, W., & Cheng, Q. (2019a). The influence of traditional Iranian and Chinese medicine on Western and Islamic countries. *Asian Journal of Medical and Biological Research*, *5*(2), 94–99. https://doi.org/10.3329/ajmbr.v5i2.42490

Shahrajabian, M. H., Sun, W., & Cheng, Q. (2019b). Traditional Chinese medicine and agriculture; organic life and sustainability for future. *GSC Biological and Pharmaceutical Sciences*, *7*(1), 91–95. https://doi.org/10.30574/gscbps.2019.7.1.0052

Sinclair, J. R. (2019). Importance of a one health approach in advancing global health security and the Sustainable Development Goals. *Revue Scientifique et Technique (International Office of Epizootics)*, *38*(1), 145–154. https://doi.org/10.20506/rst.38.1.2949

Tarasuk, V., Fafard St-Germain, A. A., & Mitchell, A. (2019). Geographic and socio-demographic predictors of household food insecurity in Canada, 2011–12. *BMC Public Health*, *19*, 12. https://doi.org/10.1186/s12889-018-6344-2

UNICEF. (2023, July). *Drinking water*. https://data.unicef.org/topic/water-and-sanitation/drinking-water/#status

The United Nations. (n.d.). *Goal 2: Zero hunger*. www.un.org/sustainabledevelopment/hunger/

United Nations Environment Programme. (n.d.). *GOAL 13: Climate action*. www.unep.org/explore-topics/sustainable-development-goals/why-do-sustainable-development-goals-matter/goal-13

U.S. Energy Information Administration. (2023, August 16). *What is energy? Sources of energy*. www.eia.gov/energyexplained/what-is-energy/sources-of-energy.php

Velazquez-Meza, M. E., Galarde-López, M., Carrillo-Quiróz, B., & Alpuche-Aranda, C. M. (2022). Antimicrobial resistance: One health approach. *Veterinary World*, *15*(3), 743–749. https://doi.org/10.14202/vetworld.2022.743-749

The World Bank Group. (n.d.). *What is food security?* www.worldbank.org/en/topic/agriculture/brief/food-security-update/what-is-food-security

World Food Program USA. (2023, March 13). *Global food crisis: 10 countries suffering the most from hunger*. www.wfpusa.org/articles/global-food-crisis-10-countries-suffering-the-most-from-hunger/

World Health Organization. (2020, December 24). *10 global health issues to track in 2021*. www.who.int/news-room/spotlight/10-global-health-issues-to-track-in-2021

World Health Organization. (2023a, September 13). *Drinking-water*. www.who.int/news-room/fact-sheets/detail/drinking-water

World Health Organization. (2023b, September 16). *Noncommunicable diseases*. www.who.int/news-room/fact-sheets/detail/noncommunicable-diseases

World Health Organization. (2023c, January 14). *Energizing health: Accelerating electricity access in health-care facilities*. www.who.int/publications/i/item/9789240066960

World Health Organization. (2023d, July 3). *One Health definitions and principles*. www.who.int/publications/m/item/one-health-definitions-and-principles

World Meteorological Organization. (n.d.). *Climate*. https://wmo.int/topics/climate

Yopa, D. S., Massom, D. M., Kiki, G. M., Sophie, R. W., Fasine, S., Thiam, O., Zinaba, L., & Ngangue, P. (2023). Barriers and enablers to the implementation of one health strategies in developing countries: A systematic review. *Frontiers in Public Health*, *11*, 1252428. https://doi.org/10.3389/fpubh.2023.1252428

Zhang, X. X., Liu, J. S., Han, L. F., Xia, S., Li, S. Z., Li, O. Y., Kassegne, K., Li, M., Yin, K., Hu, Q. Q., Xiu, L. S., Zhu, Y. Z., Huang, L. Y., Wang, X. C., Zhang, Y., Zhao, H. Q., Yin, J. X., Jiang, T. G., Li, Q., . . . & Zhou, X. N. (2022). Towards a global one health index: A potential assessment tool for one health performance. *Infectious Diseases of Poverty*, *11*(57). https://doi.org/10.1186/s40249-022-00979-9

Zhu, G., Chou, M. C., & Tsai, C. W. (2020). Lessons learned from the COVID-19 pandemic exposing the shortcomings of current supply chain operations: A long-term prescriptive offering. *Sustainability*, *12*(14), 5858. https://doi.org/10.3390/su12145858

Zoysa, M. D. (2022). Ecotourism development and biodiversity conservation in Sri Lanka: Objectives, conflicts and resolutions. *Open Journal of Ecology*, *12*(10), 638–666. https://doi.org/10.4236/oje.2022.1210037

# 5 Education Initiatives for Health Promotion and Sustainable Development

*Wang-Kin Chiu*

## Introduction

In 2015, the United Nations put forward 17 sustainable development goals (SDGs) with an extensive and comprehensive road map of interconnected targets and indicators. Encompassing a multi-dimensional perspective on sustainable development, the 17 SDGs and 169 targets have set out a global agenda to tackle various challenges and transform the contemporary world by ensuring well-being, social inclusion, economic prosperity, and quality environment (Pradhan et al., 2017; Stafford-Smith et al., 2017). Among this set of goals for global sustainability and human development, health is a fundamental component central to international development while the promotion of good physical and mental health has been widely recognised as an indispensable element in the process of moving towards a sustainable and equitable future (Bickler et al., 2020). The multiple connections of health with various SDGs, whether through direct or indirect linkages, have further reflected the complex, significant, and transformative roles of health promotion in the development of an equitable society and the realisation of the 2030 Agenda for Sustainable Development (Fortune et al., 2018).

In addition, findings from recent reports have illustrated how the fundamental health promotion principles, including rights, empowerment, and partnerships, are closely related to the SDGs while the interconnections between human rights, empowerment, and partnerships have been comprehensively examined by relevant studies and frame analysis (Haldane et al., 2019; Spencer et al., 2019). Human right to health has been increasingly advocated, and political actions are required to support the integration of health promotion and sustainable development. The general public and communities are empowered to take control over their health, while partnerships between different sectors are necessary for fruitful collaborations and initiatives to address health and social inequalities. Furthermore, there have been increasing calls for health promotion and education for sustained actions on global issues, such as climate change and sustainability (Spencer et al., 2019). Recently, the important roles of education for health promotion and the attainment of SDGs have been critically reflected (Baena-Morales & González-Víllora,

DOI: 10.4324/9781032701356-5

2023). Meanwhile, increasing reports have also discussed the important roles of education for sustainable development in the promotion of sustainable health and the attainment of SDGs (Garcia et al., 2017). It is imperative to review relevant studies in relation to health promotion and education for sustainable development for generating further insights and future directions for the development of health promotion and educational programmes.

Notably, the success of health promotion programmes relies on programme sustainability, which refers to various important aspects such as continued programme impacts, long-term maintenance of health benefits, as well as continuation of the health programmes in an organisation and within the recipient community. In this regard, this chapter will also discuss the findings from studies investigating various factors influencing the sustainability of health promotion programmes. Identifying the barriers and facilitators affecting the programme sustainability would be important for policymakers and practitioners during the design, development, and implementation of health promotion interventions to achieve sustainable health. Furthermore, recent developments in the use of technology for health promotion and educational practice for sustainable development, as well as the challenges behind it, will be discussed, with reference to reported literature and study findings, to provide further insights regarding a sustainability framework for health promotion in the post-pandemic era.

## Health Education and Health Promotion

Conventional approaches to health education, focusing on individual health risks and lifestyle choices, have encountered a paradigm shift with growing attention on a more comprehensive framework of environmental and policy interventions. In the past decade, health education has evolved considerably in content, methods, and sophistication of communication for the fulfilment of more diversified purposes and directions. Emerging new concepts of health promotion and health literacy have helped to refine the understanding of how health education can adapt to the changing landscape and public health priorities (Nutbeam, 2019; Stellefson et al., 2020a). Examining health education through the perspectives of health literacy is important in the differentiation between the traditional task-intensive approach and the evolving skills-focused health education for the development of more generic skills. Adoption of social media has been increasing in health promotion due to its advantages in the provision of accessible healthcare support and resources, particularly when physical barriers are present (Nutbeam, 2021). In recent years, health promotion has become more rooted in internet-based programmes while requiring higher competencies of health educators in the use of computer-mediated content and optimisation of consumer health experiences. Thousands of social media websites in relation to health promotion are also available to the general public (Edington et al., 2016). Advancement in social media applications has provided unprecedented opportunities for access to health information but at the same time brought new challenges to health educators (Stellefson et al.,

2020a). Health educators and health promotion practitioners are expected to be equipped with essential digital skills which include managing a vast quantity of available information and assessing the accuracy, reliability and quality of the information, in particular when considering their critical roles in designing, managing, implementing, and monitoring health promotion programmes.

In recent years, the popularity and advent of digital media have been observed in the healthcare sector (Deng et al., 2019). Social media has seen its wide applications by patients, caregivers, and healthcare professionals, with various reports suggesting its prospects in many critical issues such as patient empowerment, health promotion, and healthcare quality enhancement (Ranney & Genes, 2016; Zhang et al., 2018; Zhu et al., 2020). Meanwhile, many studies have explored the roles of social media in health promotion (Stellefson et al., 2020b). A recent review of the increasing adoption of social media for health-related intentions in low- and middle-income countries has also concluded that one of the major purposes was to facilitate health education and knowledge translation (Hagg et al., 2018). Furthermore, the study by Ghahramani et al. (2022) has reviewed the use of social media as an innovative communication and educational tool for health promotion, providing opportunities for sustainable outcomes of changing health behaviour, which is regarded as a daunting challenge in health promotion programmes. In the analysis of literature reports, the results showed that Facebook and YouTube were more frequently used for interventions to modify health behaviour while Instagram and Twitter were used more for observing the pattern and trend of health behavioural changes. Overall, it is suggested that health promotion programmes through social media have the potential in promoting sustainable changes in health behaviour.

The use of social media in health promotion programmes is an emerging field of research studies, with the significance of social resources being widely recognised as a valuable tool for promoting health behavioural changes. According to an earlier estimation, around two billion adults were either obese or overweight. The World Health Organization (WHO) has considered obesity as a global epidemic while recommending the implementation of population-wide strategies and interventions for health promotion to address the specific issues of obesity. Providing social support to individuals from salient agents in their environment is central to health promotion initiatives (Langford et al., 1997; Putland et al., 2013). A review study has reported that health promotion programmes through the use of social media could generate social support for patients and peers (Moorhead et al., 2013). Preliminary research studies have also suggested the potential of social media in enhancing participant engagement and serving as a cost-effective agent in the provision of social support to participants of weight management programmes (Jane et al., 2018). While social support is important for maintaining good health and undergoing health behavioural changes, the adoption of social media for health promotion and weight management is still in the formative stage. More research is needed to investigate the adoption of social media to augment health promotion interventions, and to elucidate the specific aspects of social media assisting overweight or obese individuals to achieve weight improvements for maximisation of potential benefits of this tool at a relatively low cost.

Furthermore, there are also other health promotion initiatives reported in the literature reflecting the use of social media for purposes of health communication and education. An interesting study has reported on the evaluation of a postgraduate assignment in which students were required to create a website for health promotion (Joseph et al., 2014). In the study, WordPress was adopted and applied as a platform for the development of students' generic and contemporary skills in the practices of health promotion. It was found that the use of web-based platforms has shown good potential in developing students' contemporary skills with regard to both health promotion and the use of social media. Social media was also reported to receive good acceptability from the student's perspective. Recently, a study by Mehmet et al. (2020) examined consumer participation and engagement with a social marketing intervention harnessing digital media. The strategic intervention was designed for supporting the implementation of Equally Well, a health promotion programme specifically aiming for improving the physical health of people living with mental issues. Meanwhile, Latha et al. (2020) have reported a qualitative study which investigated the effectiveness of social media platforms for health promotion campaigns in the context of mental health. As social media has increasingly been adopted as the platform for a rich source and vast quantity of mass communication and messages, enhancing mental health awareness with the support of social media is considered a good health promotion initiative for reaching out to many people within a short period. The study found that the Facebook and Instagram posts regarding the mental health promotion campaigns received the attention of a considerable amount of targeted populations, with an increasing trend in mental health awareness observed for the effective use of digital media platforms in disseminating health-related information.

The prevalence of sexually transmitted infections and the serious health consequences have led to significant concern in public health. The WHO has published the Global Strategy for the Prevention and Control of Sexually Transmitted Infections and the need for educating people on sexual health has been recommended and emphasised (Gabarron & Wynn, 2016). Sexual behaviour and relevant issues have aroused major public health concerns globally and effective health promotion programmes for younger groups are advocated, suggesting the use of social media as a promising platform to engage people with sexual health education (Engel, 2023). In recent years, there have been increasing studies reporting the benefits of social media interventions for sexual health promotion (Engel, 2023). Using social media as specific channels and supportive tools for the promotion of sexual health has led to positive effects on behavioural changes among the youth while there are also studies reporting a reduced incidence of positive chlamydia and gonorrhoea cases associated with social media intervention programmes (Gabarron & Wynn, 2016; Jones et al., 2012). While social media has shown good potential to support sexual health education initiatives, there is still a need for more investigations for identifying and developing strategies to effectively attract and engage users regarding the promotion of sexual health through online social networking platforms. Key strategies for successful engagement include regular personalised interaction with users, encouragement of active conversation, provision of reference links and uploading of multimedia, and highlights of celebrity involvement (Veale et al., 2015). These strategies are important for attaining significant online engagement in social networking platforms for the support of health education initiatives.

Despite its promising prospects as a health promotion tool, the dark side of harnessing social media in healthcare should not be neglected (Korda & Itani, 2013). For example, it can lead to the overconfidence of patients in making their own medical decisions (Baron & Berinsky, 2019; Smailhodzic et al., 2016). Moreover, privacy violation is a serious concern (Syed-Abdul et al., 2013). It is also noteworthy that varying levels and extent of diffusion of social media can exist among different healthcare departments and there are differences observed in the shared content and patient interactions (Jha et al., 2016; Thackeray et al., 2012). This phenomenon is probably attributable to the concern of healthcare departments over the quality of medical care delivered to patients, leading to cautious control in the adoption of social media and lagging behind other public-facing sectors (Zhu et al., 2020). Furthermore, it has been reported that unverified content has led to the sharing of misleading health-related information disseminated through video-based social media (Syed-Abdul et al., 2013). A recent review study has identified major topics of health misinformation and corresponding prevalence in different forms of social media platforms (Suarez-Lledo & Alvarez-Galvez, 2021). Six major categories, namely vaccines, smoking products and drugs, non-communicable diseases, pandemics, eating disorders, and medical treatments, have been identified based on social network analysis, content evaluation, quality evaluation, content or text analysis, and sentiment analysis. Other recent reviews have also reported the increasing prevalence and popularity of misinformation promoted in social media (Kapantai et al., 2021; Wang et al., 2019). It is recommended that more multidisciplinary collaborations are required to understand and examine the susceptibility of users. There is a prominent need for interdisciplinary approaches and research to understand and design effective actions and tools to tackle the challenges from the spread of misinformation and disinformation.

Although there has been fast growing adoption of social media in health promotion due to the removal of physical and geographical access barriers, it has also raised questions regarding health inequity for people with no or limited accessibility to the Internet or who do not use social media at all. A recent review has reported that social media interventions were effective in certain vulnerable groups such as the youth, older adults, economically disadvantaged, and rural populations, suggesting that these interventions may be effective promotion tools in the context of health equity (Welch et al., 2016). But still, confirmation of effectiveness would need more research studies to assess the health outcomes and health equity, particularly focusing on the populations at risk for disadvantage. In addition, while social media has been increasingly studied and explored as a translational tool of health promotion by integrating principles of health education and communication, in the future, more research investigations should also focus on developing effective strategies for tackling the challenges of using social media for health promotion, as well as adopting good practices and innovative methodologies in the design, implementation, and evaluation of social media forums for public health.

## Sustainability of Health Promotion Programmes

Extensive studies have investigated the implementation and effectiveness of health promotion programmes over the years (Wolfenden et al., 2016). Recently, there have been growing research studies examining the sustainability of health promotion programmes. Programme sustainability is highly important because health benefits can be maintained even after the initial implementation period. In addition, a sustainable programme is essential for maintaining community capacity, as well as optimising resources and investment (Bodkin & Hakimi, 2020). However, there are challenges to sustaining health promotion programmes arising from various reasons such as uncommon adoption of a sustainability framework as well as lack of distinct definition and poor understanding of factors influencing and promoting sustainability of health-related programmes. For effective planning and implementation of health promotion programmes with sustainable benefits, it is important to review the current practice and identify existing barriers and facilitators that inhibit or promote the sustainability of health promotion programmes.

There are growing reports of randomised controlled trials investigating the effectiveness of school-based health promotion programmes regarding a variety of health outcomes (Denford et al., 2017). Based on the findings of two systematic reviews, it is suggested that there is considerable progress in assessing the effectiveness of school-based interventions for health promotion (Bonell et al., 2013; Shackleton et al., 2016). There are other recent studies of case examples focusing on the implementation of school-based health promotion programmes (Darlington et al., 2018; Pearson et al., 2015). The study by Pearson et al. (2015) has reviewed examples of research and experience in the United Kingdom to better understand how school-based health promotion programmes can be implemented. More recently, Darlington et al. (2018) have evaluated the participation of schools in the health promotion programme "Education, Health and Territory" implemented in France between 2012 and 2015, with findings being adopted for analysing the interactions and effects of contextual factors during the implementation of health promotion programmes. While school-based health promotion has been advocated and studied extensively, a continuation of health interventions and sustaining benefits after external funding has been relatively less explored (Herlitz et al., 2020). The sustainability of school-based health promotion interventions is important. When discontinuation of effective health promotion programmes occurs, new practices cannot reach a wider population, eventually leading to wastage in the time, manpower, and resources invested for the initiation and implementation of the interventions (Scheirer & Dearing, 2011; Schell et al., 2013).

Conceptual frameworks proposed for sustainable healthcare emphasise complexity, advocating individual and collective engagement of practitioners and other actors with different intervention components and systems for intervention embedment, adaptation, and discard (Lennox et al., 2018; Wiltsey Stirman et al., 2012). Studies have also identified the important factors for promoting sustainability which include the effectiveness, attributes, and cost of interventions (Schell et al., 2013), practitioners' attributes and activities (Scheirer, 2013), and the external financial and political climate (Racine, 2006). However, when it comes to school-based health promotion and education settings, the common barriers and facilitators may be affecting the sustainability of interventions differentially. Less political incentive may be present for sustaining health interventions where academic education is usually of a higher priority (Keshavarz et al., 2010). In addition, while teachers may differ in their dedication and commitment to the nurturing of students for health promotion, it is obvious that more support and preparation time from teachers are required for the delivery of curriculums incorporating health components (Pearson et al., 2015; Tancred et al., 2018). Furthermore, inadequate or limited interaction between schools and the healthcare sector may lead to impedance in the identification of resources, funding, and training for sustainable development (Keshavarz et al., 2010).

A recent review study has suggested that the knowledge and skills of teaching staff are important in health promotion programmes while the motivation of staff is equally important in the delivery of health promotion under evolving circumstances (Herlitz et al., 2020). Take service-learning, one of the important education initiatives for health promotion, as an example. Supervision of students in service-learning subjects requires dedicated and motivated staff to provide guidance and supervision of students in conducting the services under changing situations such as in the course of pandemic outbreaks. Maintaining a dedicated team is one of the important components in the sustainable development of service-learning subjects. Many studies have suggested the promising benefits to students in health promotion, including the incorporation of health promotion knowledge and skills in providing community service to older adults, implementing service-learning educational interventions on nursing students for better community health, and adoption of experiential learning and authentic assessments for supporting students to become competent health promotion practitioners (Anderson et al., 2022; Fong et al., 2023; Marcilla-Toribio et al., 2022). More resources and manpower are worthwhile investing in service-learning subjects for developing innovative approaches and sustaining health promotion programmes.

## Education for Sustainable Development

Health, explicitly emphasised in SDG 3, is considered a core focus interconnecting with other SDGs. In addition to health promotion, integrating service-learning components in the pedagogical framework is also highly valuable to sustainable development, with growing interests and advocation of developing service-learning subjects for sustainable community development (Brower, 2011; Fong et al., 2022). Service learning is considered as a promising pedagogy to formulate a suitable model for meeting the educational needs to nurture students in addressing global challenges with regard to planetary sustainable development. Mintz et al. (2014) have reported on the design of a multidisciplinary service-learning subject aiming to introduce engineering students to concepts of sustainable development through a combination of laboratory and fieldwork activities in addition to classroom teaching. In fact, the importance of interdisciplinarity and creativity in the design and implementation of service-learning educational activities have been widely emphasised and advocated to foster students' competencies for sustainable development (Lambrechts et al., 2013; Molderez & Fonseca, 2018). The concept of interdisciplinarity was also applied in the adoption of a service-learning approach to promote students' learning for sustainable consumption (Barth et al., 2014). Moreover, service-learning has also been applied to promote other important elements of sustainable development. For example, corporate social responsibility has a significant role towards sustainable development in relation to health promotion (Chiu & Fong, 2023a). Adoption of service-learning to promote corporate social responsibility in university education can make reference to the experience of an integrated international service-learning programme incorporating the concepts of responsibility and sustainability (Pless et al., 2012).

Another global challenge requiring urgent action is the deteriorating environmental quality due to increasing levels of worldwide pollution. This is of particular concern to the growing population of older adults, which is highly vulnerable to chemical contamination and polluted environments (Chiu & Fong, 2022; Simoni et al., 2015). Recently, there have also been growing studies examining the adoption of a service-learning approach in chemistry subjects in the context of environmental sustainability (Eskew et al., 2023; Heider et al., 2018). It is noteworthy that a healthy environment is essentially important to healthy ageing particularly due to the growing trend of life expectancy and increasing cohort of older adults around the world (Fong et al., 2021). Environmental health and sustainability education initiatives are important and worth further investigation for the promotion of environmental sustainability and healthy attitudes.

Sustainability education, multidisciplinary in nature and emphasising transverse development at all societal levels for improving the planetary environment, has influential impacts on human health. It should not be restricted to any single discipline and instead, to achieve genuine attainment of sustainable development, students of diversified programmes should receive sustainability education. Estrada-Vidal and Tójar-Hurtado (2017) have conducted a survey study to investigate the knowledge and attitudes of college students in Granada. A recent study by Aleixo et al. (2021) has discussed the findings on the perceptions of students towards the integration of sustainability concepts in education and the potential impacts on health attitudes and behaviours. With the increasingly important role of higher education institutions in moving the society towards sustainable development, more studies to understand the perceptions and knowledge of diversified students regarding sustainability would be beneficial and necessary for designing and implementing effective interventions concerning environmental health and sustainability. Furthermore, recent studies have also discussed the interconnections between sustainable healthcare and education systems (Chiu & Fong, 2023b; Leung et al., 2023). More investigations are recommended for incorporating the concepts of Environmental, Social, and Governance (ESG) in education for a sustainable and healthy environment in the post-pandemic era.

Advancement of technology and the COVID-19 pandemic have led to changes in teaching and learning modalities, with surging applications of emerging technologies in education across various disciplines. Recent research and review studies have also supported that emerging digital technologies can lead to positive impacts such as enhancement in the learning experience in the education of environmental science and increased environmental awareness (Cao & Jian, 2024; Chiu, 2021). Future research directions should continue to focus on the applications of technology in education for sustainable environment and service-learning initiatives. While technology adoptions are of potential interest, it is imperative that emphasis should also be placed on pedagogical approaches. While systems thinking has been identified as a promising approach to achieving health for all in the community (Fong & Chiu, 2023), recent research has also seen impressive progress and promising prospects in the adoption of systems thinking in education for sustainable development to address the intricate nature of sustainability (Hofman-Bergholm, 2018; Koral Kordova et al., 2018). Advocations have also been put forward to call for more studies investigating the design and implementation of teaching resources for integrating systems thinking in education to nurture students' social responsibility (Chiu et al., 2022; Flynn et al., 2019).

Besides, education initiatives should also cover basic health knowledge and skills for the general public. First-aid training is beneficial to community health as injuries or accidents are significant threats to public health, which account for the leading cause of early mortality among adolescents. It has long been suggested that the implementation of school-based first-aid programmes would lead to positive impacts on students' learning of skills in reducing the severity of injury and facilitating basic life support knowledge (Maitra, 1997; Uray et al., 2003). First-aid programmes in schools also provide valuable opportunities of educating a wide spectrum of the community on fundamental first-aid skills, as well as increasing their safety awareness (Lingard, 2002; Reveruzzi et al., 2016). Furthermore, educational research has suggested that implementing early first-aid education, for example in middle childhood, may lead to benefits of enhancing interest and motivation, as well as strengthening the ability of primary school children in providing first-aid services (Bollig et al., 2009). Although many studies have supported the inclusion and practicability of first-aid training programmes in high school education and curriculum, there is still a significant need for more school-based research and programme evaluations, in particular more randomised controlled trials for the identification and development of effective practice approaches. This also applies to psychological first-aid training as mental well-being is an indispensable component of quality community health promotion.

Recently, the role of psychological first-aid in supporting mental well-being in the COVID-19 pandemic has been examined, during which the psychological conditions of the general public have been significantly affected by the fear, stress, distress, and other disorders arising from the global pandemic outbreak (Shah et al., 2020). The psychological effects of the pandemic on postsecondary students in many places such as Hong Kong have been investigated (Ng et al., 2021). During the pandemic, a task force of researchers and educators reported the development of a remote psychological first-aid intervention protocol for healthcare practitioners in a university teaching hospital in Malaysia (Sulaiman et al., 2020). There are also advocations for implementing psychological training for healthcare professionals and trainees as they are highly vulnerable to mental health distress due to various complications caused by the pandemic such as scarce life-saving resources, extreme and long working hours, isolation from family and friends for safety and health reasons, and significant risk and fear of infection (Zemel, 2022). Notably, psychological first-aid education is equally important to the general public as it also includes other vulnerable groups such as caregivers, children and older adults. Therefore, more school-based activities and incorporation of psychological first-aid knowledge in the curriculum are suggested, while more collaborations with training providers are recommended for the benefit of community health in the post-pandemic era.

## Conclusion

Sustainable health and well-being need to build on the solid foundation of effective education initiatives for health promotion and sustainable development. In this chapter, relevant studies in relation to health promotion and education for sustainable development have been reviewed for providing insights and future directions for the development of health promotion and educational programmes. Important issues in health promotion and education through social media have been reviewed and discussed. While social media has been recognised as a promising tool for sexual health education initiatives, there is still a need for more investigations to identify and develop effective strategies and interventions to attract and engage users regarding the promotion of sexual health through online networking platforms. Although there are many bright sides of adopting social media in health promotion, more investigations should also address concerns regarding health inequity for people with no or limited accessibility to the Internet or who seldom use social media. There is also a prominent need for interdisciplinary collaborations to understand and design effective interventions and resources to tackle the challenges of the spread of misinformation and disinformation.

In addition, programme sustainability is an important topic and worth more investigation in the context of health promotion so that health benefits can be maintained even after the initial implementation period. Furthermore, it is suggested more attention should be focused on the applications of technology in health promotion, education for a sustainable environment and service-learning initiatives particularly in the post-pandemic era, where the emergence of blended learning is anticipated. While technology adoptions are of promising prospects, it is imperative that emphasis should also be placed on its integration with pedagogical approaches such as systems thinking and service learning. More resources should be invested for the design of innovative approaches and sustainable development of health promotion programmes. Meanwhile, as higher education institutions play a significant role in moving the society towards sustainable development, more studies are recommended to understand the perceptions of diversified students and their knowledge of sustainability, with the goals of designing and implementing effective interventions concerning environmental health and sustainability. Furthermore, important issues of first-aid training and education have been discussed. Incorporation of first-aid knowledge in the curriculum and implementation of school-based activities are important to community health promotion and sustainable development. More studies are required for integrating the concepts of Environmental, Social and Governance (ESG) in education across different disciplines. Concerted efforts from various stakeholders including healthcare professionals, educators, students, and the community are pivotal to the success of education initiatives for sustainable health and development during the post-pandemic era.

## References

Aleixo, A. M., Leal, S., & Azeiteiro, U. M. (2021). Higher education students' perceptions of sustainable development in Portugal. *Journal of Cleaner Production*, *327*, 129429. https://doi.org/10.1016/j.jclepro.2021.129429

Anderson, K., Gupta, S., Nava Buenfil, F., & Verrinder, G. (2022). Using experiential learning and authentic assessments to support students to become competent health promotion practitioners. *Health Promotion Journal of Australia*, *33*, 27–34. https://doi.org/10.1002/hpja.654

Baena-Morales, S., & González-Víllora, S. (2023). Physical education for sustainable development goals: Reflections and comments for contribution in the educational framework. *Sport, Education and Society*, *28*(6), 697–713. https://doi.org/10.1080/13573322.2022.2045483

Baron, R. J., & Berinsky, A. (2019). Mistrust in science – a threat to the patient–physician relationship. *New England Journal of Medicine*, *381*, 182–185. https://doi.org/10.1056/nejmms1813043

Barth, M., Adomßent, M., Fischer, D., Richter, S., & Rieckmann, M. (2014). Learning to change universities from within: A service-learning perspective on promoting sustainable consumption in higher education. *Journal of Cleaner Production*, *62*, 72–81. https://doi.org/10.1016/j.jclepro.2013.04.006

Bickler, G., Morton, S., & Menne, B. (2020). Health and sustainable development: An analysis of 20 European voluntary national reviews. *Public Health*, *180*, 180–184. https://doi.org/10.1016/j.puhe.2019.05.018

Bodkin, A., & Hakimi, S. (2020). Sustainable by design: A systematic review of factors for health promotion program sustainability. *BMC Public Health*, *20*, 964. https://doi.org/10.1186/s12889-020-09091-9

Bollig, G., Wahl, H. A., & Svendsen, M. V. (2009). Primary school children are able to perform basic life-saving first aid measures. *Resuscitation*, *80*(6), 689–692. https://doi.org/10.1016/j.resuscitation.2009.03.012

Bonell, C., Jamal, F., Harden, A., Wells, H., Parry, W., Fletcher, A., Petticrew, M., Thomas, J., Whitehead, M., Campbell, R., Murphy, S., & Moore, L. (2013). Systematic review of the effects of schools and school environment interventions on health: Evidence mapping and synthesis. *Public Health Research*, *1*(1). https://doi.org/10.3310/phr01010

Brower, H. H. (2011). Sustainable development through service learning: A pedagogical framework and case example in a third world context. *Academy of Management Learning & Education*, *10*(1), 58–76. https://doi.org/10.5465/amle.10.1.zqr58

Cao, F., & Jian, Y. (2024). The Role of integrating AI and VR in fostering environmental awareness and enhancing activism among college students. *Science of the Total Environment*, *908*, 168200. https://doi.org/10.1016/j.scitotenv.2023.168200

Chiu, W. K. (2021). Pedagogy of emerging technologies in chemical education during the era of digitalization and artificial intelligence: A systematic review. *Education Sciences*, *11*(11), 709. https://doi.org/10.3390/educsci11110709

Chiu, W. K., & Fong, B. Y. F. (2022). Chemical pollution and healthy ageing: The prominent need for a cleaner environment. In V. T. S. Law & B. Y. F. Fong (Eds.), *Ageing with dignity in Hong Kong and Asia*(pp. 277–287). Springer. https://doi.org/10.1007/978-981-19-3061-4_19

Chiu, W. K., & Fong, B. Y. F. (2023a). Recent trends of research and education in ESG and sustainability. In *Environmental, social and governance and sustainable development in healthcare* (pp. 99–112). Springer. https://doi.org/10.1007/978-981-99-1564-4_7

Chiu, W. K., & Fong, B. Y. F. (2023b). Sustainable development goal 3 in healthcare. In *Environmental, social and governance and sustainable development in healthcare* (pp. 33–45). Springer. https://doi.org/10.1007/978-981-99-1564-4_3

Chiu, W. K., Fong, B. Y. F., & Ho, W. Y. (2022). The importance of environmental sustainability for healthy ageing and the incorporation of systems thinking in education for a sustainable environment. *Asia Pacific Journal of Health Management*, *17*(1), 84–89. https://doi.org/10.24083/apjhm.v17i1.1589

Darlington, E. J., Violon, N., & Jourdan, D. (2018). Implementation of health promotion programmes in schools: An approach to understand the influence of contextual factors on the process? *BMC Public Health*, *18*, 163. https://doi.org/10.1186/s12889-017-5011-3

Denford, S., Abraham, C., Campbell, R., & Busse, H. (2017). A comprehensive review of reviews of school-based interventions to improve sexual-health. *Health Psychology Review*, *11*(1), 33–52. https://doi.org/10.1080/17437199.2016.1240625

Deng, Z., Hong, Z., Zhang, W., Evans, R., & Chen, Y. (2019). The effect of online effort and reputation of physicians on patients' choice: 3-wave data analysis of china's good doctor website. *Journal of Medical Internet Research*, *21*(3), e10170. https://doi.org/10.2196/10170

Edington, D. W., Schultz, A. B., Pitts, J. S., & Camilleri, A. (2016). The future of health promotion in the 21st century: A focus on the working population. *American Journal of Lifestyle Medicine*, *10*(4), 242–252. https://doi.org/10.1177/1559827615605789

Engel, E. (2023). Young peoples' perceived benefits and barriers of sexual health promotion on social media-a literature review. *International Journal of Health Promotion and Education*, 1–20. https://doi.org/10.1080/14635240.2023.2241035

Eskew, N. A., Smythers, A. L., & Hutson, B. L. (2023). Research and service learning in a garden of chemistry. *Journal of Chemical Education*, *100*(11), 4395–4405. https://doi.org/10.1021/acs.jchemed.3c00246

Estrada-Vidal, L. I., & Tójar-Hurtado, J. C. (2017). College student knowledge and attitudes related to sustainability education and environmental health. *Procedia-Social and Behavioral Sciences*, *237*, 386–392. https://doi.org/10.1016/j.sbspro.2017.02.030

Flynn, A. B., Orgill, M., Ho, F. M., York, S., Matlin, S. A., Constable, D. J., & Mahaffy, P. G. (2019). Future directions for systems thinking in chemistry education: Putting the pieces together. *Journal of Chemical Education*, *96*(12), 3000–3005. https://doi.org/10.1021/acs.jchemed.9b00637

Fong, B. Y. F., & Chiu, W. K. (2023). A systems approach to achieving health for all in the community. In B. Y. F. Fong & W. C. W. Wong (Eds.), *Gaps and actions in health improvement from Hong Kong and Beyond* (pp. 41–54). Springer. https://doi.org/10.1007/978-981-99-4491-0_4

Fong, B. Y. F., Chiu, W. K., Chan, W. F. M., & Lam, T. Y. (2021). A review study of a green diet and healthy ageing. *International Journal of Environmental Research and Public Health*, *18*(15), 8024. https://doi.org/10.3390/ijerph18158024

Fong, B. Y. F., Ng, T. K. C., Yee, H. H. L., & Chow, B. S. M. (2022). Ageing with dignity through service-learning – Hong Kong experience. In V. T. S. Law & B. Y. F. Fong (Eds.), *Ageing with dignity in Hong Kong and Asia: Holistic and humanistic care* (pp. 347–359). Springer. https://doi.org/10.1007/978-981-19-3061-4_24

Fong, B. Y. F., Yee, H. H. L., Ng, T. K. C., & Chiu, W. K. (2023). Intergenerational service-learning: An experience in health promotion among undergraduate students in Hong Kong. *Journal of Intergenerational Relationships*, 1–14. https://doi.org/10.1080/15350770.2023.2172514

Fortune, K., Becerra-Posada, F., Buss, P., Galvão, L. A. C., Contreras, A., Murphy, M., Rogger, C., Keahon, G. E., & de Francisco, A. (2018). Health promotion and the agenda for sustainable development, WHO Region of the Americas. *Bulletin of the World Health Organization*, *96*(9), 621. https://doi.org/10.2471%2FBLT.17.204404

Gabarron, E., & Wynn, R. (2016). Use of social media for sexual health promotion: A scoping review. *Global Health Action*, *9*(1), 32193. https://doi.org/10.3402/gha.v9.32193

Garcia, J., da Silva, S. A., Carvalho, A. S., & de Andrade Guerra, J. B. S. O. (2017). Education for sustainable development and its role in the promotion of the sustainable development goals. In J. Davim (Eds.), *Curricula for sustainability in higher education* (pp. 1–18). Springer. https://doi.org/10.1007/978-3-319-56505-7_1

Ghahramani, A., de Courten, M., & Prokofieva, M. (2022). The potential of social media in health promotion beyond creating awareness: An integrative review. *BMC Public Health*, *22*, 2402. https://doi.org/10.1186/s12889-022-14885-0

Hagg, E., Dahinten, V. S., & Currie, L. M. (2018). The emerging use of social media for health-related purposes in low and middle-income countries: A scoping review. *International Journal of Medical Informatics*, *115*, 92–105. https://doi.org/10.1016/j.ijmedinf.2018.04.010

Haldane, V., Chuah, F. L., Srivastava, A., Singh, S. R., Koh, G. C., Seng, C. K., & Legido-Quigley, H. (2019). Community participation in health services development, implementation, and evaluation: A systematic review of empowerment, health, community, and process outcomes. *PLoS ONE*, *14*(5), e0216112. https://doi.org/10.1371/journal

Heider, E. C., Valenti, D., Long, R. L., Garbou, A., Rex, M., & Harper, J. K. (2018). Quantifying sucralose in a water-treatment wetlands: Service-learning in the analytical chemistry laboratory. *Journal of Chemical Education*, *95*(4), 535–542. https://doi.org/10.1021/acs.jchemed.7b00490

Herlitz, L., MacIntyre, H., Osborn, T., & Bonell, C. (2020). The sustainability of public health interventions in schools: A systematic review. *Implementation Science*, *15*, 4. https://doi.org/10.1186/s13012-019-0961-8

Hofman-Bergholm, M. (2018). Could education for sustainable development benefit from a systems thinking approach? *Systems*, *6*(4), 43. https://doi.org/10.3390/systems6040043

Jane, M., Hagger, M., Foster, J., Ho, S., & Pal, S. (2018). Social media for health promotion and weight management: A critical debate. *BMC Public Health*, *18*, 932. https://doi.org/10.1186/s12889-018-5837-3

Jha, A., Lin, L., & Savoia, E. (2016). The use of social media by state health departments in the US: Analyzing health communication through Facebook. *Journal of Community Health*, *41*, 174–179. https://doi.org/10.1007/s10900-015-0083-4

Jones, K., Baldwin, K. A., & Lewis, P. R. (2012). The potential influence of a social media intervention on risky sexual behavior and Chlamydia incidence. *Journal of Community Health Nursing*, *29*(2), 106–120. https://doi.org/10.1080/07370016.2012.670579

Joseph, E., Hinga, A., Roberts, K., Pearce, M., Buckley, T., de Viggiani, N., & Jones, M. (2014). Health promotion in the age of social media: Evaluation of Word Press as a platform for developing postgraduate student skills. *British Journal of Education, Society & Behavioural Science*, *4*(9), 1274–1289. https://doi.org/10.9734/BJESBS/2014/10583

Kapantai, E., Christopoulou, A., Berberidis, C., & Peristeras, V. (2021). A systematic literature review on disinformation: Toward a unified taxonomical framework. *New Media & Society*, *23*(5), 1301–1326. https://doi.org/10.1177/1461444820959296

Keshavarz, N., Nutbeam, D., Rowling, L., & Khavarpour, F. (2010). Schools as social complex adaptive systems: A new way to understand the challenges of introducing the health promoting schools concept. *Social Science & Medicine*, *70*(10), 1467–1474. https://doi.org/10.1016/j.socscimed.2010.01.034

Koral Kordova, S., Frank, M., & Nissel Miller, A. (2018). Systems thinking education – Seeing the forest through the trees. *Systems*, *6*(3), 29. https://doi.org/10.3390/systems6030029

Korda, H., & Itani, Z. (2013). Harnessing social media for health promotion and behavior change. *Health Promotion Practice*, *14*(1), 15–23. https://doi.org/10.1177/1524839911405850

Lambrechts, W., Mulà, I., Ceulemans, K., Molderez, I., & Gaeremynck, V. (2013). The integration of competences for sustainable development in higher education: An analysis of bachelor programs in management. *Journal of Cleaner Production*, *48*, 65–73. https://doi.org/10.1016/j.jclepro.2011.12.034

Langford, C. P. H., Bowsher, J., Maloney, J. P., & Lillis, P. P. (1997). Social support: A conceptual analysis. *Journal of Advanced Nursing*, *25*(1), 95–100. https://doi.org/10.1046/j.1365-2648.1997.1997025095.x

Latha, K., Meena, K. S., Pravitha, M. R., Dasgupta, M., & Chaturvedi, S. K. (2020). Effective use of social media platforms for promotion of mental health awareness. *Journal of Education and Health Promotion*, *9*, 124. https://doi.org/10.4103%2Fjehp.jehp_90_20

Lennox, L., Maher, L., & Reed, J. (2018). Navigating the sustainability landscape: A systematic review of sustainability approaches in healthcare. *Implementation Science*, *13*, 27. https://doi.org/10.1186/s13012-017-0707-4

Leung, T. C. H., Chiu, W. K., You, C. S. X., & Fong, B. Y. F. (2023). Sustainable development in healthcare through an environmental, social and governance approach. In *Environmental, social and governance and sustainable development in healthcare* (pp. 1–9). Springer. https://doi.org/10.1007/978-981-99-1564-4_1

Lingard, H. (2002). The effect of first aid training on Australian construction workers' occupational health and safety motivation and risk control behavior. *Journal of Safety Research*, *33*(2), 209–230. https://doi.org/10.1016/S0022-4375(02)00013-0

Maitra, A. (1997). School accidents to children: Time to act. *Journal of Accident & Emergency Medicine*, *14*(4), 240–242. https://doi.org/10.1136%2Femj.14.4.240

Marcilla-Toribio, I., Moratalla-Cebrián, M. L., Bartolomé-Guitierrez, R., Cebada-Sánchez, S., Galán-Moya, E. M., & Martínez-Andrés, M. (2022). Impact of service-learning educational interventions on nursing students: An integrative review. *Nurse Education Today*, *116*, 105417. https://doi.org/10.1016/j.nedt.2022.105417

Mehmet, M., Roberts, R., & Nayeem, T. (2020). Using digital and social media for health promotion: A social marketing approach for addressing co-morbid physical and mental health. *Australian Journal of Rural Health*, *28*(2), 149–158. https://doi.org/10.1111/ajr.12589

Mintz, K., Talesnick, M., Amadei, B., & Tal, T. (2014). Integrating sustainable development into a service-learning engineering course. *Journal of Professional Issues in Engineering Education and Practice*, *140*(1), 05013001. https://doi.org/10.1061/(ASCE)EI.1943-5541.0000169

Molderez, I., & Fonseca, E. (2018). The efficacy of real-world experiences and service learning for fostering competences for sustainable development in higher education. *Journal of Cleaner Production*, *172*, 4397–4410. https://doi.org/10.1016/j.jclepro.2017.04.062

Moorhead, S. A., Hazlett, D. E., Harrison, L., Carroll, J. K., Irwin, A., & Hoving, C. (2013). A new dimension of health care: Systematic review of the uses, benefits, and limitations of social media for health communication. *Journal of Medical Internet Research*, *15*(4), e85. https://doi.org/10.2196/jmir.1933

Ng, T. K. C., Fong, B. Y. F., Yee, H. H. L., & Law, V. T. S. (2021). Psychological effects of COVID-19 pandemic among postsecondary students in Hong Kong: A mixed methods research. *Asia Pacific Journal of Public Health*, *33*(8), 932–934. https://doi.org/10.1177/10105395211032820

Nutbeam, D. (2019). Health education and health promotion revisited. *Health Education Journal*, *78*(6), 705–709. https://doi.org/10.1177/0017896918770215

Nutbeam, D. (2021). From health education to digital health literacy–building on the past to shape the future. *Global Health Promotion*, *28*(4), 51–55. https://doi.org/10.1177/17579759211044079

Pearson, M., Chilton, R., Wyatt, K., Abraham, C., Ford, T., Woods, H. B., & Anderson, R. (2015). Implementing health promotion programmes in schools: A realist systematic review of research and experience in the United Kingdom. *Implementation Science*, *10*, 149. https://doi.org/10.1186/s13012-015-0338-6

Pless, N. M., Maak, T., & Stahl, G. K. (2012). Promoting corporate social responsibility and sustainable development through management development: What can be learned from international service learning programs? *Human Resource Management*, *51*(6), 873–903. https://doi.org/10.1002/hrm.21506

Pradhan, P., Costa, L., Rybski, D., Lucht, W., & Kropp, J. P. (2017). A systematic study of sustainable development goal (SDG) interactions. *Earth's Future*, *5*(11), 1169–1179. https://doi.org/10.1002/2017EF000632

Putland, C., Baum, F., Ziersch, A., Arthurson, K., & Pomagalska, D. (2013). Enabling pathways to health equity: Developing a framework for implementing social capital in practice. *BMC Public Health*, *13*, 517. https://doi.org/10.1186/1471-2458-13-517

Racine, D. P. (2006). Reliable effectiveness: A theory on sustaining and replicating worthwhile innovations. *Administration and Policy in Mental Health and Mental Health Services Research*, *33*(3), 356–387. https://doi.org/10.1007/s10488-006-0047-1

Ranney, M. L., & Genes, N. (2016). Social media and healthcare quality improvement: A nascent field. *BMJ Quality & Safety*, *25*(6), 389–391. https://doi.org/10.1136/bmjqs-2015-004827

Reveruzzi, B., Buckley, L., & Sheehan, M. (2016). School-based first aid training programs: A systematic review. *Journal of School Health*, *86*(4), 266–272. https://doi.org/10.1111/josh.12373

Scheirer, M. A. (2013). Linking sustainability research to intervention types. *American Journal of Public Health, 103*(4), e73–e80. https://doi.org/10.2105/AJPH.2012.300976

Scheirer, M. A., & Dearing, J. W. (2011). An agenda for research on the sustainability of public health programs. *American Journal of Public Health, 101*(11), 2059–2067. https://doi.org/10.2105/AJPH.2011.300193

Schell, S. F., Luke, D. A., Schooley, M. W., Elliott, M. B., Herbers, S. H., Mueller, N. B., & Bunger, A. C. (2013). Public health program capacity for sustainability: A new framework. *Implementation Science, 8*, 15. https://doi.org/10.1186/1748-5908-8-15

Shackleton, N., Jamal, F., Viner, R. M., Dickson, K., Patton, G., & Bonell, C. (2016). School-based interventions going beyond health education to promote adolescent health: Systematic review of reviews. *Journal of Adolescent Health, 58*(4), 382–396. https://doi.org/10.1016/j.jadohealth.2015.12.017

Shah, K., Bedi, S., Onyeaka, H., Singh, R., & Chaudhari, G. (2020). The role of psychological first aid to support public mental health in the COVID-19 pandemic. *Cureus, 12*(6). https://doi.org/10.7759/cureus.8821

Simoni, M., Baldacci, S., Maio, S., Cerrai, S., Sarno, G., & Viegi, G. (2015). Adverse effects of outdoor pollution in the elderly. *Journal of Thoracic Disease, 7*(1), 34. https://doi.org/10.3978/j.issn.2072-1439.2014.12.10

Smailhodzic, E., Hooijsma, W., Boonstra, A., & Langley, D. J. (2016). Social media use in healthcare: A systematic review of effects on patients and on their relationship with healthcare professionals. *BMC Health Services Research, 16*, 442. https://doi.org/10.1186/s12913-016-1691-0

Spencer, G., Corbin, J. H., & Miedema, E. (2019). Sustainable development goals for health promotion: A critical frame analysis. *Health Promotion International, 34*(4), 847–858. https://doi.org/10.1093/heapro/day036

Stafford-Smith, M., Griggs, D., Gaffney, O., Ullah, F., Reyers, B., Kanie, N., Stigson, B., Shrivastava, P., Leach, M., & O'Connell, D. (2017). Integration: The key to implementing the Sustainable Development Goals. *Sustainability Science, 12*, 911–919. https://doi.org/10.1007/s11625-016-0383-3

Stellefson, M., Paige, S. R., Chaney, B. H., & Chaney, J. D. (2020a). Evolving role of social media in health promotion: Updated responsibilities for health education specialists. *International Journal of Environmental Research and Public Health, 17*(4), 1153. https://doi.org/10.3390/ijerph17041153

Stellefson, M., Paige, S. R., Chaney, B. H., & Chaney, J. D. (2020b). Social media and health promotion. *International Journal of Environmental Research and Public Health, 17*(9), 3323. https://doi.org/10.3390/ijerph17093323

Suarez-Lledo, V., & Alvarez-Galvez, J. (2021). Prevalence of health misinformation on social media: Systematic review. *Journal of Medical Internet Research, 23*(1), e17187. https://doi.org/10.2196/17187

Sulaiman, A. H., Ahmad Sabki, Z., Jaafa, M. J., Francis, B., Razali, K. A., Juares Rizal, A., Mokhtar, N. H., Juhari, J. A., Zainal, S., & Ng, C. G. (2020). Development of a remote psychological first aid protocol for healthcare workers following the COVID-19 pandemic in a university teaching hospital, Malaysia. *Healthcare, 8*, 228. https://doi.org/10.3390/healthcare8030228

Syed-Abdul, S., Fernandez-Luque, L., Jian, W. S., Li, Y. C., Crain, S., Hsu, M. H., Wang, Y. C., Khandregzen, D., Chuluunbaatar, E., Nguyen, P. A., & Liou, D. M. (2013). Misleading health-related information promoted through video-based social media: Anorexia on YouTube. *Journal of Medical Internet Research, 15*(2), e30. https://doi.org/10.2196/jmir.2237

Tancred, T., Paparini, S., Melendez-Torres, G. J., Fletcher, A., Thomas, J., Campbell, R., & Bonell, C. (2018). Interventions integrating health and academic interventions to prevent substance use and violence: A systematic review and synthesis of process evaluations. *Systematic Reviews, 7*, 227. https://doi.org/10.1186/s13643-018-0886-3

Thackeray, R., Neiger, B. L., Smith, A. K., & Van Wagenen, S. B. (2012). Adoption and use of social media among public health departments. *BMC Public Health, 12*, 242. https://doi.org/10.1186/1471-2458-12-242

Uray, T., Lunzer, A., Ochsenhofer, A., Thanikkel, L., Zingerle, R., Lillie, P., Brandl, E., & Sterz, F. (2003). Feasibility of life-supporting first-aid (LSFA) training as a mandatory subject in primary schools. *Resuscitation, 59*(2), 211–220. https://doi.org/10.1016/S0300-9572(03)00233-8

Veale, H. J., Sacks-Davis, R., Weaver, E. R., Pedrana, A. E., Stoové, M. A., & Hellard, M. E. (2015). The use of social networking platforms for sexual health promotion: Identifying key strategies for successful user engagement. *BMC Public Health, 15*, 85. https://doi.org/10.1186/s12889-015-1396-z

Wang, Y., McKee, M., Torbica, A., & Stuckler, D. (2019). Systematic literature review on the spread of health-related misinformation on social media. *Social Science & Medicine, 240*, 112552. https://doi.org/10.1016/j.socscimed.2019.112552

Welch, V., Petkovic, J., Pardo, J. P., Rader, T., & Tugwell, P. (2016). Interactive social media interventions to promote health equity: An overview of reviews. *Health Promotion and Chronic Disease Prevention in Canada: Research, Policy and Practice, 36*(4), 63–75. https://doi.org/10.24095%2Fhpcdp.36.4.01

Wiltsey Stirman, S., Kimberly, J., Cook, N., Calloway, A., Castro, F., & Charns, M. (2012). The sustainability of new programs and innovations: A review of the empirical literature and recommendations for future research. *Implementation Science, 7*, 17. https://doi.org/10.1186/1748-5908-7-17

Wolfenden, L., Williams, C. M., Wiggers, J., Nathan, N., & Yoong, S. L. (2016). Improving the translation of health promotion interventions using effectiveness–implementation hybrid designs in program evaluations. *Health Promotion Journal of Australia, 27*(3), 204–207. https://doi.org/10.1071/HE16056

Zemel, R. (2022). A COVID-19 call to action: Psychological first aid training for medical professionals and trainees. *Academic Psychiatry, 46*(6), 769–773. https://doi.org/10.1007/s40596-022-01645-w

Zhang, W., Deng, Z., Evans, R., Xiang, F., Ye, Q., & Zeng, R. (2018). Social media landscape of the tertiary referral hospitals in China: Observational descriptive study. *Journal of Medical Internet Research, 20*(8), e249. https://doi.org/10.2196/jmir.9607

Zhu, C., Xu, X., Zhang, W., Chen, J., & Evans, R. (2020). How health communication via Tik Tok makes a difference: A content analysis of Tik Tok accounts run by Chinese provincial health committees. *International Journal of Environmental Research and Public Health, 17*(1), 192. https://doi.org/10.3390/ijerph17010192

# 6 Lifelong Health Promotion for All

*Ethel S. T. Sha and Ben Y. F. Fong*

## Introduction

The World Health Organization (WHO) has defined health promotion as a "process of enabling people to increase control over and to improve their health", emphasising that health promotion concerns not only enhancing an individual's skills and capabilities to have better health but also the impacts on the social, environmental, and economic determinants of health to achieve a better population health (WHO, 2021). Therefore, health promotion requires individual efforts to live a healthy lifestyle and the resultant collective contributions to lay a firm foundation for sustainable health improvement and, thus, its promotion.

The Ottawa Charter (WHO, 1986) (the Charter) is considered the milestone document in the development of health promotion after the Declaration of Alma-Ata in 1978. Three aims of health promotion were suggested in the Charter: creating favourable conditions for health, achieving equity in health for all people, and concerting efforts from all sectors and people from all walks of life through the mediation of varying interests in society. To reach the aims of health promotion, the Charter set out five action areas:

(1) **Establishment of healthy public policy**: seeking health equity via law, budgetary constraints, taxes, and organisational reforms while considering the obstacles to and solutions for implementing such policies in non-health sectors.
(2) **Creation of supportive environments**: assisting individuals in leading stimulating, enjoyable lives and careers while preserving the built and natural environments and natural resources.
(3) **Reinforcement of community action**: enabling the communities via adequate information access, health education opportunities, and financial support to improve self-help and social support.
(4) **Developing personal skills**: requiring actions from and within educational, professional, commercial, and volunteer organisations to provide individuals with information, health-related knowledge, and life skills in the

DOI: 10.4324/9781032701356-6

workplace, family, and community to make healthier decisions, deal with chronic illnesses and injuries, and better prepare for various life stages.

(5) **Reorientation of health services**: emphasising intersectoral responsibilities, focusing more on health research, and alterations in professional development result in an attitudinal and organisational change in health services to adopt a holistic view of the needs of individuals.

Health promotion requires collaboration between health and non-health sectors to ensure individuals, communities, and the planet live healthily throughout their lifespan. The life course approach considers the needs of different age groups and uses a comprehensive framework for interventions and knowledge translation (Department of Health [DH], 2008; Health Bureau, 2023a; Mikkelsen et al., 2019). As suggested by recent reports, adopting a systems thinking approach helps understand the interdependence of health systems and the complex interactions between biological endowment, health behaviours, social networks, family influences, and socioeconomic conditions to achieve health for all in the community (de Savigny & Adam, 2009; Fong, 2022; Wagner et al., 2024). Hence, this approach can target non-communicable diseases at their roots and allow timely intervention at specific points in the life cycle, reducing disability and premature deaths (DH, 2008; Edelman & Kudzma, 2022; Mikkelsen et al., 2019). Effective promotion of health and controlling primary risk factors in early life can maintain adult functions and independence and prevent disability in older life (DH, 2008; Mikkelsen et al., 2019).

## Current Practices of Health Promotion in Hong Kong

City-wide health promotion and disease prevention guidelines are praised for protecting people from behavioural risk and non-communicable diseases (Strid et al., 2022). In Hong Kong, health policies have considered the needs of Hong Kong citizens of all ages, from prenatal to elderhood, ensuring health promotion strategies are suited to the needs of different life stages. To formulate and execute the policies, Hong Kong's healthcare system comprises public and private services, with the Health Bureau being responsible for developing policies and resource distribution to manage health services and ensure the effective execution of public health promotion and protection, and the Department of Health for implementation of policies and legislation to protect public health through services such as health promotion (HKSAR Government, 2023a). Nevertheless, community involvement and empowerment and individual efforts are essential for reaching certain health objectives, and the Health Promotion Branch plays a crucial role in this (DH, 2021).

In 2008, the Government initiated a strategic framework to prevent and manage non-communicable diseases, which engaged representatives from various sectors to discuss and supervise the implementation plan. In 2018, "Towards 2025: Strategy and Action Plan to Prevent and Control

Non-communicable Diseases in Hong Kong" was published with the objectives of preventing and controlling non-communicable diseases by 2025, and the mascot "Lazy Lion" was introduced along with various media promotions such as television announcements, press releases, radio programmes, public events, and flash mob performances, focusing on alcohol reduction, physical activities, and prevention of cancers.

The Government released the Primary Healthcare Blueprint in December 2022 to address issues related to service delivery, governance, resources, manpower and technology of the healthcare system in building a primary healthcare system that can improve the overall health of the people and enhance their quality of life (Health Bureau, 2022). Subsequently, the Life Course Preventive Care Plan, an evidence-based, comprehensive health strategy emphasising disease prevention and personalised health needs across different life stages, was launched in 2023. The plan is one of the Hong Kong reference frameworks in primary healthcare. It guides healthcare professionals and enhances public awareness of self-health management and healthy lifestyles (Health Bureau, 2023a).

The Department of Health (2008) suggested a three-tier prevention model for health promotion programmes:

(1) **Primary prevention:** To prevent illnesses from arising by promoting changes in behaviour through health education, vaccination, environmental interventions, and social policies (DH, 2008). In June 2005, a territory-wide programme called "2 plus 3 a Day" was initiated to increase public awareness of a balanced diet. Health messages were spread through mass media, leaflets, and recipe distribution. Exhibition boards included posters, a 24-hour health education hotline, a website, and various events.

(2) **Secondary prevention:** Halting the advancement of an illness by timely identification and diagnosis, and subsequent swift and efficient treatment (DH, 2008). Screening is a commonly established type of secondary prevention. The cervical cancer screening programme was implemented in March 2004, followed by the colorectal cancer screening programme after the 2014 Policy Address.

(3) **Tertiary prevention**: Enhancing quality of life and reducing complications after disease diagnosis through services like cardiac rehabilitation in both public and private sectors to improve patients' functional capacity, reduce risk factors, and instil a sense of well-being and hope for the future (DH, 2008).

### *Health Promotion for the Childbearing Period*

Prior to pregnancy, family planning is essential. The WHO's Director of the Department of Sexual and Reproductive Health (SRH), including the UNDP-UNFPA-UNICEF-WHO-World Bank Special Programme of Research, Development and Research Training in Human Reproduction (HRP), Professor Pascale Allotey said, "Family planning promotes self-actualisation, empowerment, as well as health and well-being, and reduces maternal and infant deaths through the prevention of unintended pregnancy and unsafe abortion". Given this significance, the Family Planning Association of Hong Kong (www.famplan.org.hk) (FPAHK), formerly the Eugene League founded in 1936, provides birth control services and public information on family planning in Hong Kong, as well as clinic and counselling services in Sexual and Reproductive Health, and public education and research. The Family Health Service (FHS) of the Department of Health runs Family Planning Services at selected Maternal and Child Health Centres (MCHCs), empowering women to autonomously and conscientiously determine the quantity and timing of their offsprings.

The Maternal Health Service under FHS covers the healthcare of women during the prenatal and postnatal phases of pregnancy. Pregnant women visit MCHCs for regular check-ups, blood tests, pregnancy-related health education, pre-recorded FAQs, and advice on feeding infants and young children. Additionally, they can receive personalised therapy to adjust to postpartum life changes. Leaflets on antenatal care are available to provide pregnant women with the necessary information to lead healthy lives for themselves and their children in the womb, including a healthy diet, oral health, harms of second-hand and third-hand smoke, and transmissible diseases. This period is a family-centred health promotion opportunity in which family members have to reduce their use of tobacco and alcohol as well as minimise air pollution within the home environment (Mikkelsen et al., 2019).

Exclusive breastfeeding aids in preventing non-communicable diseases and promotes optimal neonatal development. This practice necessitates governmental policies that endorse and facilitate it, such as labour rules mandating universal paid maternity leave and businesses providing appropriate facilities for nursing mothers (Mikkelsen et al., 2019). In 2017, the Department of Health issued a policy paper on supporting and promoting breastfeeding, which listed the advantages of breastfeeding and ways to create a supportive environment for implementing this policy. Following the issuance of the policy paper, a series of TV announcements, leaflets, audio-visual resources, and posters were disseminated to promote and advocate breastfeeding practice to families and the society. Also, government premises started to provide baby care facilities, and the Buildings Department (2018) released a practice notice encouraging construction professionals to include infant care facilities for the public and lactation rooms for staff in private commercial buildings.

### *Health Promotion for Infants, Toddlers, and Preschool Children*

"An ounce of prevention is better than a pound of cure". Health promotion and prevention are undoubtedly beneficial and should be started very early in life. Children with good health will develop fewer chronic diseases and enjoy life more with families, schools, peers and sports (Australian Institute of Health and Welfare, 2024). Therefore, health promotion starting in infancy is vital, and it is a crucial time for scheduled vaccinations to combat infections in the community. To improve children's environmental determinants of health, their exposure to harmful influences, such as secondary tobacco smoke and air pollution, should be minimised (Mikkelsen et al., 2019).

Furthermore, training in healthy daily living, such as diet and feeding, regular exercise and outdoor activities, social communication, politeness, safety, and hygienic social habits such as hand washing, cleanliness, proper disposal of rubbish, and restricted screen time must be introduced by the parents and carers at home and teachers at the nurseries and kindergartens. All the health promotional activities must be adequately and strictly guided by parents and supported by teachers with the heart and a loving and personal touch to be effective and long-lasting for the health and well-being of the children at this critical time of life.

The Child Health Service under FHS operates a comprehensive child health and development plan at MCHCs for children aged from birth to five years old, with the aim of enhancing overall health and wellness. The main elements of the plan consist of parenting, vaccination, and health and development monitoring. The parenting curriculum prepares parents to raise healthy and well-adjusted children, addressing physical and mental health aspects. Besides, the Hong Kong Childhood Immunisation Programme attempts to safeguard young children from 11 infectious illnesses, including Tuberculosis, Hepatitis B, Diphtheria, Tetanus, Pertussis, Poliovirus, Pneumococcal, Measles, Mumps, Rubella, and Varicella. Children aged 0 to 18 months should receive immunisations to avoid common and non-communicable diseases in the future. The vaccination coverage for babies born in 2021 was predicted to exceed 95% for the specified vaccines (DH, 2023b). Also, the FHS operates the Health and Developmental Surveillance Programme, which focuses on partnership with parents, teachers, and other caregivers, intending to facilitate parents and caregivers to be competent and effective in promoting and observing children's development, with health professionals involved in regular assessments to detect children's health and developmental issues (DH, 2023d).

### *Health Promotion for School-Age Children and Adolescents*

Education and monitoring of body weight among children and adolescents are essential in avoiding obesity and its consequences of compromised health for this age group. Meanwhile, a balanced diet is equally essential for their growth and body development. Furthermore, attention to hearing and visual health will help to detect impairment of the two crucial senses needed for learning at school. Children and adolescents must be taught to protect their ears and eyes through the proper use of sound and visual equipment, particularly ear speakers, headphones, and smartphones, as well as enjoying sensible screen time (Health Bureau, 2023a). A health-promoting school environment and practice can encourage children to adopt a healthy lifestyle and protect their health (Mikkelsen et al., 2019). The Global School Health Initiative, launched by WHO in 1995, utilised schools as a platform to enhance the health of children and families. This is well adopted by the Student Health Service of the Department of Health (2023a) to establish a conducive environment for living, studying, and working within schools.

In 2019, the Health Promoting School Programme was initiated as a trial in 30 local schools in Hong Kong to assist schools in creating health promotion plans and striving to establish a healthy campus. This initiative focused on six key factors: healthy school policies, physical environment, social environment, community connections, skills for healthy living, and health care and promotion services within the school. The programme was then extended as the "Whole School Health Programme" in the 2023/24 school year, adopting a whole-school approach to deliver comprehensive health information and establish long-term development (HKSAR Government, 2023b). It focuses on healthy diet, physical activity, mental health and social well-being of students, and sustainability of health promotion in school settings.

As children grow, they learn to make independent decisions about health and lifestyle; hence, improving health literacy is crucial at this stage (Mikkelsen et al., 2019). A wide range of health information is available for students and teachers on the website of Student Health Service, including healthy living, diet and nutrition, physical exercise, sex education, psychosocial health, addictive behaviour, learning, career choice, and responsible utilisation of the internet and smart gadgets. In addition, an elective subject for the Hong Kong Diploma of Secondary Education Examination, Health Management and Social Care, has been offered to senior secondary school students in some schools since 2009. The syllabus is comprehensive, intending to equip students with the knowledge to lead a healthy lifestyle later in life. The course material is readily available on the website for reference (Education Bureau, 2016). Students not taking the elective subject have access to the information as well.

During this stage of life, prioritising mental health and wellness is crucial by focusing on preventing bullying and offering school-based support, counselling, and therapy (Mikkelsen et al., 2019). Following the previous student guidance services, the Education Bureau launched the "One School Social Worker for Each School" policy for primary schools in the 2018/19 school year. For secondary schools, the Government has been supporting this service since the 1970s, and the Social Welfare Department implemented the "Two School Social Workers for Each School" in the 2019/20 school year to provide support and counselling for secondary school students. In response to the social unrest in 2019 and the ongoing COVID-19 epidemic, the Government allocated \$300 million from the Beat Drugs Fund to launch the "Mental Health Initiatives Funding Scheme" in July 2021 and June 2022. This initiative aimed to enhance support for individuals in the community experiencing mental health challenges and to increase public awareness about mental health. The Social Welfare Department funded 24 Integrated Community Centres for Mental Wellness to offer clinical services and educational programmes to secondary school students in specific districts. These services were provided by non-governmental organisations (NGOs) and self-financed mental health services.

Other government departments are also working with NGOs to raise awareness among secondary school students about the use of harmful substances, such as drugs, alcohol, and tobacco. For example, the Narcotics Division of the Security Bureau established the Beat Drugs Fund in 1996 to encourage and support anti-drug initiatives, especially among the youth and to enhance community-wide activities and programmes to combat drug abuse in Hong Kong. The Fund has initiated a school-based campaign called Healthy School Programme with a Drug Testing Component. This programme aims to strengthen students' determination to avoid drugs, cultivate an anti-drug environment in schools, and encourage those struggling with drug issues to seek assistance.

Vaccination remains vital for primary school children as a public health measure and a health promotion strategy. The outreaching School Immunisation Teams of the Department of Health perform vaccination at primary schools. In addition to MMRV and DtaP-IPV vaccines for all Primary 1 and Primary 6 students, eligible female primary school students are also given the human papillomavirus (HPV) vaccine as part of the Hong Kong Childhood Immunisation Programme, since the 2019/20 school year. Providing HPV vaccines to adolescents is cost-effective when included in a complete strategy for cervical cancer prevention (Mikkelsen et al., 2019).

### *Health Promotion for Young and Middle-Aged Adults*

The workplace is a suitable, convenient, and crucial environment for health promotion (Law, 2020). However, it is commonly overlooked by policymakers, employers, trade unions, and the public. Health and safety are often managed and promoted together for the working population. In Hong Kong, the Occupational Safety and Health Council (www.oshc.org.hk/eng/main/about_us/oshc_profile/) is a statutory body established in 1988 to promote occupational safety and health at work and in the community to sustain the valuable workforce of Hong Kong. It is also responsible for education and training, consultancy, development of research and strategies, information dissemination, facilitating exchanges between the government, employers, employees, professionals and academics. The Labour Department also offers occupational safety and health services to enforce, educate, and promote workplace safety and health, including the Occupational Safety and Health Ordinance (CAP 509).

Safety in the workplace, particularly those involving the use of machinery and labour force, should be cautiously and strictly observed. Industrial accidents causing lives are not uncommon. Protection for workers must be a top priority for employers, senior management, and unit supervisors. On the other hand, many contemporary offices are desk-bound, leading employees to have extended periods of sitting and inadequate physical exercise (Close et al., 2018). In addition, demands for some positions, particularly senior management, job instability, and excessive workloads pose a hazard to the health of employees (Charkhabi, 2018; Hagqvist et al., 2018; Law, 2020). According to a survey by City Mental Health Alliance Hong Kong (2022), more than 50% of participants had symptoms of anxiety, despair, apathy, and excessive worrying. Workplaces should prioritise and promote mental health and well-being. The Department of Health, the Labour Department, and the Occupational Safety and Health Council have collaborated to introduce the "Joyful@Healthy Workplace" initiative. It aims to provide a favourable work environment for employers and workers, promoting healthy nutrition, physical exercise, and mental health. Companies in the scheme have access to workshops, advice services, training courses, and toolkits for health assessments.

To promote the well-being and healthy lifestyle of these age groups, the Department of Health has established the Woman Health Service and initiated the Men's Health Programme to enhance the health of women and men in Hong Kong. Women under 64 years old are eligible for health assessment services for common chronic diseases, physical examinations, health education, individual counselling on healthy lifestyle promotion, and cancer prevention. Adult men can access useful information on men's health issues through various resources provided by the Government, such as the website, travelling exhibitions, pamphlets, and brochures. These resources offer health tips on maintaining a healthy lifestyle, quitting smoking and substance abuse, caring for one's family, and seeking medical advice to enhance one's well-being. It is also crucial to monitor alcohol and tobacco consumption to avoid related diseases from the consumption of these products (Mikkelsen et al., 2019). Regular risk assessment for chronic or degenerative conditions and screening for cancers are generally included in bodycheck packages widely available in the private sector, either paid out of pocket or by employers as a staff benefit. Publicly funded schemes, like cervical cancer, breast cancer, colorectal cancer screening programmes, and the chronic disease co-care scheme, are also available to eligible residents.

The Government extended statutory paid maternity leave from ten weeks to 14 weeks in July 2020 to align with International Labour Organization standards. An observational study on 1,414 respondents, with a mean age of 32 and mostly working in skilled occupations, before and two years after the policy implementation has shown that the new leave entitlement was associated with a 22 per cent decrease in postnatal depressive symptoms and a 33 per cent decrease in postpartum emotional well-being interference among the new mothers, most of whom were primiparous. The findings amount to significant mental health benefits in the improvement of mental wellness for women in this age group and help to retain them in the workforce (Andres et al., 2024).

Moreover, mid-life crisis often affects individuals aged between 40 and 60 years. Individuals in this age group are frequently required to fulfil various personal and social responsibilities within their homes and workplaces, which might involve potential hazards in striving to achieve their objectives and requirements (Wahrendorf et al., 2013). They experience anxiousness, restlessness, discontentment with life, and a strong urge for substantial life alterations. Experiencing unstable work or involuntary joblessness in mid-life might lead to the development of depression symptoms later on (Wahrendorf et al., 2013).

Attention is drawn to the equity issue in these age groups in the life course, particularly the disparity in financial situation and affordability for health services. In order to achieve health equity, it is essential to implement health-promoting interventions in various accessible contexts, such as community centres and recreational facilities. Additionally, budgetary measures are required to support those facing disadvantages. Income is a significant stressor and contributor to health disparities among employed individuals, particularly those living in a high-cost urban environment. Working poverty in Hong Kong is exacerbated by high living costs, especially housing expenses, leading to increased deprivation of resources and materials for many individuals (CUHK Institute of Health Equity, 2022). The Government has initiated several schemes to assist unemployed or low-income adults in achieving health equity, including the "Comprehensive Social Security Assistance (CSSA) Scheme" from the Social Welfare Department and the "Re-employment Training Programme for the Middle-aged" from the Labour Department. However, the Government, healthcare professionals, social work professionals, academia, and community groups are not focusing enough on avoiding or addressing mid-life crises. Local literature on this issue is scarce, with the exception of a study conducted by Shek in 1996, which was over 30 years ago. No information or conversation can be located on social media platforms. The stakeholders, especially the Government and NGOs, should advocate for the well-being and contentment of middle-aged individuals, who occupy pivotal and influential positions in managing and influencing all aspects of our society.

### *Health Promotion for Older Adults*

During the journey from adulthood to retirement, individuals undergo significant and often irreversible shifts in identities and connections, potentially resulting in social isolation, grief, and financial strain (Mikkelsen et al., 2019). Furthermore, as individuals age, they experience a rise in physical and cognitive limitations, leading to a decline in their intrinsic capacity and subjective well-being (Lum, 2020). With the increasing health needs, it is crucial to have suitable policies, effective care delivery, appropriate rehabilitation, and easy access to support services like community centres, primary healthcare programmes, assisted living facilities, hospitals, and home care services to aid in older adults' independent living and allow for ageing in place (Lum, 2020; Mikkelsen et al., 2019; Fong & Law, 2017). In particular, promoting good health and well-being for older adults after COVID-19 is a top priority agenda for all governments, advocated by recent articles discussing about healthy ageing from the personal, social, economic, public health, and political perspectives during the post-pandemic era. Elderly residents in nursing homes were more susceptible to infectious infections and psychological problems during the pandemic due to a lack of protective gear, limited social contact, and the open layout of the facilities (Ng & Law, 2024).

In 1998, the Department of Health created the Elderly Health Service for people aged 65 and older, offering clinic, outreach, public health, and administration services. The programme seeks to improve primary healthcare for elderly individuals in the community by enhancing their self-care skills, promoting healthy lifestyles, and bolstering family support. Health promotion activities are regularly conducted at the 18 Elderly Health Centres to educate participants about prevalent health concerns in older individuals, life planning for the latter stages of life, maintaining a good diet, ensuring safety, and using Health Care Vouchers. Additionally, 18 health teams provide outreach services in the community and residential care settings. They conduct health promotion activities for older individuals and their carers in partnership with other elderly service providers.

Regarding the sustainable development goals laid out by the United Nations, healthy ageing is particularly related to SDG 3, concerning people's good health and well-being (Fong et al., 2021). The Hong Kong SAR Government has introduced a number of strategies to respond to the SDGs. The Government has distributed various guidelines and taken different measures to reduce communicable and non-communicable diseases for older adults to age healthily in place, for example, the Patient Empowerment Programme for patients with diabetes launched in 2010, the Colorectal Cancer Screening Programme piloted in 2016, the "Hong Kong Reference Framework for Diabetes Care for Adults in Primary Care Settings", revised in 2023 (Health Bureau, 2023b), and the "Guidelines on Prevention of Communicable Diseases in Residential Care Homes for the Elderly", reviewed in 2023 (DH, 2023c). As indicated in target 3.4 of SDG 3, the mental health and well-being of older adults are of major concern, particularly after the COVID-19 pandemic (Fong et al., 2021). The Hong Kong mental morbidity survey for older people found that 8.6% of elderly respondents living at home developed depression and anxiety disorders due to multiple chronic diseases and inadequate physical and social activities (Faculty of Medicine, CUHK, 2023). In view of the prevalent needs for older adults' mental wellness, the Hong Kong Jockey Club Charities Trust initiated the "JC JoyAge: Jockey Club Holistic Support Project for Elderly Mental Wellness" (https://research.jcjoyage.hk) to line up District Elderly Community Centres (DECCs) and Integrated Community Centre for Mental Wellness (ICCMW) for enhancing older adults' resilience on a community basis. In target 3.8 of SDG 3, universal health coverage is emphasised. In addition to equitable access to healthcare irrespective of socioeconomic status, CSSA, Old Age Allowance, Old Age Living Allowance, the Elderly Health Care Voucher Scheme, and the Government Vaccination Programme are available to support older adults in achieving health equity (Fong et al., 2021).

### *Other Health Promotional Activities in the Community*

The Hospital Authority, which manages all public hospitals in Hong Kong, promotes health by arranging exhibitions, workshops, and health promotion activities via the Health InfoWorld in collaboration with community partners, professionals, companies, patient organisations, and volunteers (DH, 2008). Through Patient Resources Centres (www.ha.org.hk/visitor/ha_visitor_text_index.asp?Content_ID=10083&Lang=ENG&Dimension=100) and Health Resource Centres (www3.ha.org.hk/ntec/content/hrc_e.asp), together with the General and Specialist Out-patient Clinics, the Hospital Authority offers health education, community engagement, and promotion of self-care and self-management to the general community.

NGOs and statutory bodies are essential partners in health promotion through all life course stages, involving healthcare and non-healthcare professionals, such as social workers, teachers, and counsellors. They actively organise health education activities, promote well-being, research, and engage in community practices. In recent years, professionals in Chinese medicine have become more involved in health promotion. The Chinese Medicine Regulatory Office of the Department of Health (www.cmro.gov.hk/) provides ample information on health maintenance and herbal and food tonics on its website to promote physical and mental health from the Chinese Medicine perspective to the public. District Health Centres, Chinese Medicine clinics of the universities, Hong Kong Clinical Chinese Medicine Practitioners Association, and other NGOs organise health talks on Chinese Medicine.

However, differences in assumptions or epistemological positions may create tensions in the transdisciplinary approach when conceptualising health promotion by different disciplines (Pineo et al., 2021). Transdisciplinary teams in health promotion practices and research may face challenges from long project durations, obtaining adequate research funding for projects, and problems in communication within and beyond team members (Pineo et al., 2021).

## Community Care Practitioners – the Case in Hong Kong

Recognising the necessary role that NGOs play in promoting health in an ageing society, the Hong Kong Jockey Club Charities Fund created a "Healthcare for Good" track under their initiated and funded programme called "JC PROcruit C" (https://jcprocruitc.org.hk/en) in 2020. It was a traineeship programme that supported fresh graduates transitioning from school to work. Tung Wah Group of Hospitals (TWGHs), one of the four convenors in the "Healthcare for Good" track, has created the job role of Community Care Practitioner (CCP) since 2021. This role was designed mainly because of the increasing demand for the workforce in primary healthcare and the emerging workforce options of fresh graduates. Candidates of CCPs had different education attainment and training disciplines, including social sciences, health science, business, and arts. They were assigned to various social service units in 2022/23. Those in 2023/24 were mainly assigned to elderly community centres, emphasising dementia care. A few were assigned to primary schools to support the Health Promoting School Programme. The variety of their backgrounds has been found to have enriched the delivery of social services.

Prior to their assignment, CCPs were equipped with the necessary skills and knowledge in a series of onboarding and on-the-job training in fundamental services for target service users. To better prepare CCPs to work in their settings, TWGHs trained CCPs with practical skills and specific knowledge, including common health problems and needs of primary school students and older persons, the care needs and required skills, and basic knowledge of health indicators.

CCPs at primary schools worked alongside teachers and social workers to conduct programmes and activities to teach primary students about stress management, anger management and emotion management, and healthy diet and physical activity, covering students' physical and mental health promotion. Given teachers' heavy workloads and limited support, this standalone job role for health promotion was increasingly important at schools for students' health (Youth I.D.E.A.S., 2021). A recent annual health assessment of 233,000 primary students and 97,000 secondary students, conducted by the Department of Health's Student Health Service in the 2022/23 school year, showed that one in five students was experiencing an overweight problem, and 2.8% (about 9,240 students) planned to commit suicide and 1.3% (about 4,290 students) attempted suicide in the past 12 months (HKSAR Government, 2024). The findings were alarming and dedicated manpower for health promotion at schools is necessary.

CCPs at elderly community centres mainly worked for older adults and their caregivers. These CCPs worked with health professionals and social workers to provide all-round health promotion services, including cognitive training and social support activities, which would not only consider the older adults' physical and mental health but also create a supportive environment in managing the social determinants of health of the older adults and their caregivers. Their job role and functions were similar to those of Environmental Health Officers (EHOs) in British Columbia, Canada (Campbell et al., 2011).

According to the ongoing programme evaluation conducted by the Hong Kong Institute of Asia-Pacific Studies (HKIAPS) at the Chinese University of Hong Kong, 100% of the service users were willing to seek help or services from CCPs and were satisfied with the service provided by the CCPs (W. Ho, personal communication, 17 April 2024). CCPs' presence was proven helpful in health promotion in a community setting.

A Case Report:

> *A CCP who majored in psychology provided mental health talks at his elderly community centre. The elderly participants found his talks informative and helpful, which allowed them to understand the epistemology, symptoms and prevention methods of various mental health issues. Moreover, the talks provided information on where to get support and how to care for people struggling with mental health issues. His employer also recorded the*

*talks for future health promotion and appreciated his efforts, 'We realised the prevalence of mental health issues among the elderly population and the significance of addressing this health problem in the community. We were glad that our Community Care Practitioner shared the professional knowledge from his psychology study in all these mental health talks to enhance our members' and the public's awareness and understanding of mental health issues'. Another centre supervisor also appreciated the CCPs; they helped much in cognitive training and home visits, which supplemented the centre with the necessary workforce and gave elderly users cross-generational care.*

Given the diverse backgrounds of CCPs, health promotion work was not limited to providers of certain educational and professional backgrounds. CCPs could also provide the necessary information to promote health awareness and literacy if they received the fundamental training to understand common health issues and prevention measures. It signified that CCPs could assist health promotion by working with healthcare professionals. This approach could effectively expand the talent pool of community health practitioners to respond to the rising demand for human resources in the healthcare sector, notably when the Hong Kong Government launched the primary healthcare blueprint in 2022.

## The Way Forward

Different departments of the Hong Kong government are working on different determinants of health for all age groups to provide a better environment for health and wellness, as well as health promotion as recommended by the WHO. Although there are detailed structures and strategies for health promotion, it is essential to highlight that endorsement and backing from leadership at all levels are crucial for carrying out and maintaining evidence-based healthcare practices (Strid et al., 2022). Effective advocacy, enabling policy structures, and public engagement are essential for sustainable health promotion practices (Barry, 2021).

### *Coherence of Health Promotion Strategies*

For Hong Kong to achieve transformative health promotion for the community, all sectors must align their policies, systems, and actions with the values, principles, and health promotion strategies. Collaborative leadership across disciplines is necessary to enhance mutual engagement and establish a shared vision and comprehension of health promotion to develop cooperative and purposeful solutions (Leinonen & Syväjärvi, 2022). Enhancing cross-disciplinary leadership requires administrators to have the right mindset, behaviours, and administrative culture. Additionally, policy commitment, ministerial responsibility, territory-wide action plans with clear goals, accountability mechanisms, governance structure, and a competent workforce for health promotion are all crucial factors (Barry, 2021; Leinonen & Syväjärvi, 2022).

To achieve sustainable and equitable human development, governance, and decision-making at all levels should prioritise anti-poverty programmes, universal health coverage, and effective health promotion policies (Hancock, 2011). Correct and informed decisions, thus, need to be made by sectors other than healthcare, including all government and non-government sectors, and private and community sectors, setting their health goals and targets with considerations of the determinants of health, such as income, education, and employment, and with innovation (Wise & Signal, 2000). Physical and social structures in the communities and governance processes should be modified to cater for local needs and the environment when necessary. The healthcare system should be re-oriented to create more environmentally sustainable and socially engaging communities and focus more on quality primary care so that people can make healthy choices the easy choice to enhance their self-care capability (Hancock, 2011).

### *Increase in Investment in Health Promotion*

More investments in innovative research methods and strengthening essential health promotion functions are highly recommended, including effective prevention and control, sound advocacy for health, enabling policy structures for cross-sectoral health promotion actions, implementation systems, and workforce capacity building (Barry, 2021; Hancock, 2011). For example, the government can implement fiscal policies to increase taxes on unhealthy items like tobacco, alcohol, and sugary beverages. The revenue generated can then support initiatives subsidising fruits and vegetables, as well as health promotion (Mikkelsen et al., 2019).

However, it must be remembered that financial incentives for consumers alone are inadequate to promote primary care or public-private partnerships that are conducive to health promotion (Schoeb, 2016). Sufficient time, reimbursement, education, health literacy, counselling skills, and stakeholders' involvement are also crucial in preventing non-communicable diseases, implementing strategies, and changing health behaviours among the public and healthcare professionals (Strid et al., 2022).

### *Ongoing Evaluation of Health Promotion Programmes*

For the quality and sustainability of health promotion, systematic follow-up and audit of health promotion programmes are needed (Ader et al., 2001). Consumer quality, professional quality, and management quality provide a balanced view of how well a health promotion programme has been carried out by comparing the public's expectations and experience, the professionals' planning and designing of health promotion programmes, and the cost and higher-level directives (Øvretveit, 1996). Additionally, programmes' structures, processes, and outcomes should be tested using various indicators (Ader et al., 2001). Practically, evaluating the impact of a community intervention on long-term health and social outcomes is challenging due to the complexity involved in tracing the causal relationship. Triangulation can enhance trust in study results by applying it to data collecting, researchers, and research procedures (Nutbeam, 1998).

Additionally, practitioners may need to evaluate specific components to optimise the efficacy of health promotion programmes, as institutional modifications are frequently necessary. The adaptability of the initiative to the internal context, the time allocated for institutionalising change, the deliberate inclusion of short-term success in the implementation plan by change agents, the overall group experience of action for change, and the resources available to agencies for focusing on internal factors are vital factors to consider (Batras et al., 2016).

#### *Extended Pool of Talents for Health Promotion*

The example of Community Care Practitioners illustrates that non-professionals, who are fresh graduates from non-healthcare disciplines, can initiate and implement health promotion programmes in the community. Concerning the roles and functions of EHOs in British Columbia and the increasing demand for workforce in primary care, the Government, in collaboration with NGOs like the Hong Kong College of Community Health Practitioners (www.hkcchp.org/), can consider developing similar positions in Hong Kong, such as Community Health Practitioners, to concentrate on improving health via enhancing personal abilities, establishing supportive surroundings, and aiding in the establishment and implementation of healthy public policies (Campbell et al., 2011).

## References

Ader, M., Berensson, K., Carlsson, P., Granath, M., & Urwitz, V. (2001). Quality indicators for health promotion programmes. *Health Promotion International, 16*(2), 187–195. https://doi.org/10.1093/heapro/16.2.187

Andres, E. B., Du, X., Pang, S. S. L., Liang, J. N., Ye, J., Lee, M. H., Tarrant, M., Yung, S. S., Johnston, J. M., Lok, K. Y. W., & Quan, J. (2024). Extended paid maternity leave associated with improved maternal mental health in Hong Kong. *Health Affairs (Project Hope), 43*(5), 707–716. https://doi.org/10.1377/hlthaff.2023.00742

Australian Institute of Health and Welfare. (2024). *Health of children*. www.aihw.gov.au/reports/children-youth/health-of-children

Barry, M. M. (2021). Transformative health promotion: What is needed to advance progress?. *Global Health Promotion, 28*(4), 8–16. https://doi.org/10.1177/17579759211013766

Batras, D., Duff, C., & Smith, B. J. (2016). Organizational change theory: Implications for health promotion practice. *Health Promotion International, 31*(1), 231–241. https://doi.org/10.1093/heapro/dau098

Buildings Department. (2018). *Practice note for authorized persons, registered structural engineers and registered geotechnical engineers (ADV-32): Provision of babycare rooms and lactation rooms in commercial buildings*. https://www.bd.gov.hk/doc/en/resources/codes-and-references/practice-notes-and-circular-letters/pnap/ADV/ADV032.pdf

Campbell, A. C., Foggin, T. M., Elliott, C. T., & Kosatsky, T. (2011). Health promotion as practised by public health inspectors: The BC experience. *Canadian Journal of Public Health – Revue Canadienne de sante publique, 102*(6), 432–436. https://doi.org/10.1007/BF03404194

Charkhabi, M. (2018). Do cognitive appraisals moderate the link between qualitative job insecurity and psychological-behavioral well-being?. *International Journal of Workplace Health Management, 11*(1), 424–441. https://doi.org/10.1108/IJWHM-01-2018-0008.

City Mental Health Alliance Hong Kong. (2022). *Mental health and well-being in the workplace: Survey of Hong Kong employees.* www.cmhahk.org/docs//Research/Employee-Survey-Report-2022-(ENG).pdf

Close, M. A., Lytle, L. A., Viera, A. J., Chen, D., Linnan, L. A., & Valle, C. G. (2018). Identifying and describing segments of office workers by activity patterns: Associations with demographic characteristics and objectively measured physical activity. *International Journal of Workplace Health Management, 11*(1), 16–30. https://doi.org/10.1108/IJWHM-07-2017-0053.

CUHK Institute of Health Equity. (2022). *Health inequalities in Hong Kong: A life course approach.* www.instituteofhealthequity.org/resources-reports/health-inequalities-in-hong-kong-a-life-course-approach/full-report.pdf

Department of Health. (2008). *Promoting health in Hong Kong: A strategic framework for prevention and control of non-communicable diseases.* https://www.change4health.gov.hk/filemanager/common/image/strategic_framework/promoting_health/promoting_health_e.pdf

Department of Health. (2021). *Health promotion branch, main service areas.* Department of Health. www.dh.gov.hk/english/main/main_chp/health.html

Department of Health. (2023a). *Whole school health programme.* Student Health Service. www.studenthealth.gov.hk/english/hps/hps_info/info.html

Department of Health. (2023b). *Health facts of Hong Kong* (2023 ed.). www.dh.gov.hk/english/statistics/statistics_hs/files/2023.pdf

Department of Health. (2023c). *Guidelines on prevention of communicable diseases in residential care homes for the elderly.* www.chp.gov.hk/files/pdf/guidelines_on_prevention_of_ communicable_diseases_in_rche_eng.pdf

Department of Health. (2023d). *Developmental surveillance scheme.* Family Health Service. www.fhs.gov.hk/english/health_info/child/13033.html

De Savigny, D., & Adam, T. (Eds.). (2009). *Systems thinking for health systems strengthening.* Alliance for Health Policy and Systems Research, WHO. https://iris.who.int/handle/10665/44204

Edelman, C. L., & Kudzma, E. C. (2022). *Health promotion throughout the life span*(10th ed.). Elsevier.

Education Bureau. (2016). *Health management and social care.* https://cd.edb.gov.hk/tc/hmsc/eng/index.aspx

Faculty of Medicine, CUHK. (2023, November 29). *CUHK announces survey results on the mental health of local child, adolescent and elderly populations* [Press release]. https://www.med.cuhk.edu.hk/press-releases/cuhk-announces-survey-results-on-the-mental-health-of-local-child-adolescent-and-elderly-populations

Fong, B. Y. F. (2022). *Systems thinking and sustainable healthcare delivery* (1st ed.). Routledge. https://doi.org/10.4324/9781003305637

Fong, B. Y. F., & Law, V. T. S. (2017). Aging in place. In B. Fong, A. Ng, & P. Yuen (Eds.), *Sustainable health and long-term care solutions for an aging population* (pp. 259–276). IGI Global. https://doi.org/10.4018/978-1-5225-2633-9.ch014

Fong, B. Y. F., Law, V. T. S., Leung, T. C. H., Lo, M. F., Ng, T. K. C., & Yee, H. H. L. (2021). Ageing and sustainable development goal 3 in Hong Kong. In B. Y. F, Fong & V. T. S. Law (Eds.), *Sustainable Development Goal 3: Health and well-being of ageing in Hong Kong* (1st ed., pp. 22–43). Routledge. https://doi.org/10.4324/9781003220169-2

Hagqvist, E., Vinberg, S., Landstad, B. J., & Nordenmark, M. (2018). Is the gap between experienced working conditions and the perceived importance of these conditions related to subjective health? *International Journal of Workplace Health Management*, *11*(1), 2–15. https://doi.org/10.1108/IJWHM-08-2017-0067

Hancock, T. (2011). Health promotion in Canada: 25 years of unfulfilled promise. *Health Promotion International*, *26*(S2), ii263–267. https://doi.org/10.1093/heapro/dar061

Health Bureau. (2022). *Primary healthcare blueprint*. https://www.primaryhealthcare.gov.hk/bp/en/index.html

Health Bureau. (2023a). *Life course preventive care for general public*. https://www.healthbureau.gov.hk/pho/main/life_course_preventive_care_for_all.html?lang=2

Health Bureau. (2023b). *Hong Kong reference framework for diabetes care for adults in primary care settings*. https://www.healthbureau.gov.hk/phcc/rfs/src/pdfviewer/web/pdf/diabetescare/en/16_en_RF_DM_full.pdf

HKSAR Government. (2023a). *Overview of the health care system in Hong Kong*. https://www.gov.hk/en/residents/health/hosp/overview.htm

HKSAR Government. (2023b). *DH to promote "whole school, whole health" (with photos)* [Press release]. https://www.info.gov.hk/gia/general/202306/29/P2023062900467.htm

HKSAR Government. (2024, January 3). *DH announces key findings of annual health assessment of Student Health Service* [Press Release]. https://www.info.gov.hk/gia/general/202401/03/P2024010300236.htm

Law, V. (2020). Health-promoting workplaces. In B. Fong, V. Law & A. Lee (Eds.), *Primary care revisited*(pp. 115–134). Springer. https://doi.org/10.1007/978-981-15-2521-6_8

Leinonen, J., & Syväjärvi, A. (2022). Barriers to health promotion strategy work in Finnish municipalities. *Health Promotion International*, *37*(3), daac091. https://doi.org/10.1093/heapro/daac091

Lum, C. M. (2020). Primary care for older adults. In B. Fong, V. Law, & A. Lee (Eds.), *Primary care revisited*(pp. 175–188). Springer. https://doi.org/10.1007/978-981-15-2521-6_11

Mikkelsen, B., Williams, J., Rakovac, I., Wickramasinghe, K., Hennis, A., Shin, H.-R., Rarmer, M., Berdzull, N., Borges, C., Huber, M., & Breda, J. (2019). Life course approach to prevention and control of non-communicable diseases. *BMJ (Clinical research ed.)*, *364*, l257. https://doi.org/10.1136/bmj.l257

Ng, T. C. K., & Law, V. T. S. (2024). Worldwide impacts on aged care during and after the COVID-19 pandemic. In W. Chiu & V. T. S. Law (Eds.), *Healthy ageing after COVID-19: Research and policy perspectives from Asia* (1st ed., pp. 35–48). Routledge. https://doi.org/10.4324/9781003436881

Nutbeam, D. (1998). Evaluating health promotion – progress, problems and solutions. *Health Promotion International*, *13*(1), 27–44. https://doi.org/10.1093/heapro/13.1.27

Øvretveit, J. (1996). Quality in health promotion. *Health Promotion International*, *11*(1), 55–62.

Pineo, H., Turnbull, E. R., Davies, M., Rowson, M., Hayward, A. C., Hart, G., Johnson, A. M., & Aldridge, R. W. (2021). A new transdisciplinary research model to investigate and improve the health of the public. *Health Promotion International*, *36*(2), 481–492. https://doi.org/10.1093/heapro/daaa125

Schoeb, V. (2016). Healthcare service in Hong Kong and its challenges: The role of health professionals within a social model of health. *China Perspectives*, *2016*(4), 51–58. https://doi.org/10.4000/chinaperspectives.7118

Shek, D. T. L. (1996). Midlife crisis in Chinese men and women. *The Journal of Psychology*, *130*(1), 109–119. https://doi.org/10.1080/00223980.1996.9914993

Strid, E. N., Wallin, L., & Nilsagård, Y. (2022). Implementation of a health promotion practice using individually targeted lifestyle interventions in primary health care: Protocol for the "Act in Time" mixed methods process evaluation study. *JMIR Research Protocols*, *11*(8), e37634. https://doi.org/10.2196/37634

Wagner, C., Carmeli, C., Jackisch, J., Kivimäki, M., van der Linden, B. W. A., Cullati, S., & Choiolero, C. (2024). Life course epidemiology and public health. *The Lancet Public Health*, *9*(4), E261–E269. https://doi.org/10.1016/S2468-2667(24)00018-5
Wahrendorf, M., Blane, D., Bartley, M., Dragano, N., & Siegrist, J. (2013). Working conditions in mid-life and mental health in older ages. *Advances in Life Course Research*, *18*(1), 16–25. https://doi.org/10.1016/j.alcr.2012.10.004
Wise, M., & Signal, L. (2000). Health promotion development in Australia and New Zealand. *Health Promotion International*, *15*(3), 237–248. https://doi.org/10.1093/heapro/15.3.237
World Health Organization. (1986). *Ottawa Charter for health promotion, 1986*. World Health Organization.
World Health Organization. (2021). *Health promotion glossary of terms 2021*. World Health Organization.
Youth I.D.E.A.S. (2021). *Supporting teachers in facing educational challenges*. Youth Research Centre, the Hong Kong Federation of Youth Groups. https://yrc.hkfyg.org.hk/wp-content/uploads/sites/56/2021/04/YI059_Report.pdf

# Index

Printed in the United States
by Baker & Taylor Publisher Services